NEW BEGINNINGS
IN SEARCH OF SELF

By

Cathy Brochu

ISBN: 1-4140-2550-5 (e-book)
ISBN: 1-4140-2551-3 (Paperback)

This book is printed on acid free paper.

1stBooks – rev. 01/13/04

Also by Cathy Brochu

Lost Innocence
A Daughter's Account of Love, Fear and
Desperation

Acknowledgments

A special thank you to Pam Walker, for her countless hours, time and energy spent on reediting the manuscript.

To Mary Constance Egan, thank you for believing in me.

To Tim and Sandy Strack, for their assistance with the picture taking and helping me create the book cover. Thank you!

And lastly, to God/Goddess. From whom, my strength, endurance, perseverance, love and faith are drawn.

Dedication

This book is dedicated to a woman who shared much of her wisdom with me, who shared much of her life with me. We journeyed down life's path for many years with one another, learning, growing, laughing and sharing tears of joy and sadness. She was one of those rare unexplainable gifts that life has to offer. Isabell Dailey Conklin, the impact that you have had on my life has had a profound effect. Thank you!

From The Readers

" New Beginnings is a poignant, and accurate description of the emotional and psychological struggles most incest victims face, but doesn't end there. Cathy takes the reader through her journey of overcoming her compelling fears, her anguish, her sadness, shame and anger by maintaining a clear sense of purpose and optimism about how life should be. She allows herself to be open and connected to people who are capable of safe and nurturing relationships and aid in her quest for feelings of self worth.

Not only does Cathy's book give hope to other victims and professionals in the field, but also provides a clear message for perpetrators in identifying the issues they need to address and what questions they need to answer to help their victims. I am delighted to be able to use this book as a significant tool in my private practice."

Cheryl Klier Karpinski, A.C.S.W.
Syracuse, New York

" New Beginnings is more than just the title to a good book. It is a guidepost to the rest of the world as lived by Cathy Brochu. Turning page after page, the reader is witness not to a cauldron of crying and self-flagellation, but a celebration of success. Discovered in this story's written words is a moving account of how one person overcame hurdles that would have dissuaded even the most hearty of individuals. No one would want to live through the incredibly difficult times that were visited upon Cathy at an early age. However all of us would hope that we would experience the joy, the happiness, and the self-contentment that was eventually had by Cathy. It did not come easy. It came, I can only assume, as the result of the efforts of a self-directed, incredibly focused young lady. Bravo!"

Ralph A. Cognetti, Esq.
Syracuse, New York

" The author is a woman of strength and courage who has written a compelling book from first hand experience. Her journey is truly uplifting. For anyone who works in the field this is a must read."

Nick Pallotta, MSW
Syracuse, New York

" New Beginnings is a compelling addition to the powerful story shared in "Lost Innocence." Cathy has a unique ability to make the reader feel as if s/he is experiencing the events of Cathy's life along with her. In this book, Cathy reminds all of us of the difference unconditional love can make in the lives of those around us. I am grateful to Cathy for her courage and her vision and look forward eagerly to the final installment of the trilogy."

Randi Bregman
Executive Director of Vera House, Inc.
Syracuse, New York

" The voice of a resilient survivor jumps off the pages of <u>New Beginnings: In Search of Self</u> and invites the reader to embark on the painful journey from trauma to recovery. In the sequel to <u>Lost Innocence</u> the child's voice grows from adolescence to adulthood and her strength is resounding. Through her struggles, the author evolves from victim to victim advocate and leaves a legacy of hope and healing for all children who have been abused."

Jennifer Cornish Genovese, ACSW, CSW
Psychotherapist, specializing in the treatment of
Traumatized children
Syracuse, New York

437-1686
6315 Fley Rd E, Syr.

" In New Beginnings, we are invited into a journey of healing that makes us want to turn the page – will the author be able to overcome the confusion and deep wounds that are the legacy of her incestuous family history? Will she be able to open her heart and let love in? Will she find her path in this world? We want to know the answers to these questions and we are not disappointed. The accounts of her emotional, psychological and spiritual healing and the "angels" who come along to help her are uplifting. Anyone reading this book will be inspired to move forward through areas of their own wounded ness and into their own new beginnings."

Cherie Ackerson, MS, LMT
Body – centered psychotherapist and body worker
Syracuse, New York

" This book examines the next chapter in the life of Cathy Brochu. You need not have experienced her first book **LOST INNOCENCE** to understand **NEW BEGINNINGS.**

This is outstanding reading and easy to understand – I recommend it to any person who has gone through a purgatory like that experienced by Cathy Brochu. Ms. Brochu shares information that is intimate and wise. If nothing else, the reader will see that greatness and success can come even from ashes if a person has the will to persevere.

Teachers, counselors, therapist, judges, lawyers and anyone who has an interest in family law will find Brochu's book invaluable in their work. The professionals who read this book will be better able to help their clients cope and succeed."

Karen J. Doctor, M.A., M.S.
Attorney & Counselor at Law
Syracuse, New York

" What an amazing and incredible journey Cathy Brochu has taken and has been able to share with us. What a profound impact she has made on those who have read her works as well as on those she has served as a professional in our community. In New Beginnings Cathy shows that there is hope for victims, survivors and for those who work with the many who suffer from abuse. Driven by faith and a will to move on Cathy finally feels the self worth and peace that she deserves. She clearly shows that if one has faith, one can find love, the kind of love that does not hurt."

Cheryl Kadlubowski, B.A.
Community Service Provider
Syracuse, New York

" Heartwarming, painful, an exceptional journey by an exceptional woman. Her heartfelt journey gives hope and inspiration for others.

A truly intimate and personal means of sharing. A communication of the wide spectrum of emotions that are normal for the recovery process.

This book is truly a support and encouragement to those who have experienced abuse and are ready to put their shoes on and walk through the dark to the light to a new beginning."

Joan Marie Myers, CSW-R, ACSW
Child and Adolescent Therapist
Syracuse, New York

" In New Beginnings, Cathy Brochu has chronicled a painful story of childhood sexual abuse that seems to have become much too familiar in recent years. Ms. Brochu's journey is often sad and depressing, but ultimately one of hope for the future – hers and ours. Her resilience and will to make a satisfying place for herself in the world is admirable, if not heroic. This is a book that should be read to understand how child sexual abuse happens and, just as importantly, how to stop it from happening."

Steve Forrester, Esq.
Child Welfare Attorney
New York, New York

Table of Contents

Author's Notes

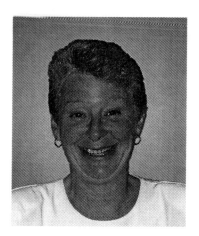

In the first part of the trilogy, **Lost Innocence**, the author shares with the reader a life-affirming experience of recovery and a sense of hope that all victimized children can reclaim their lives and esteem following trauma. In the second part of the trilogy, **New Beginnings**, you will journey with the author as she shares how it was possible through the exploration and integration of self, risk taking, relationship building and sheer determination was able to make a difference in her own life as well as the lives of other's.

Chapter One

Missing

Syracuse Herald Journal, October 15, 1970

MISSING: Catherine Ann Brochu, 16, of 320 Gertrude Street
has been reported missing since
early Monday morning. She is
described as 5 feet 5 inches tall,
100 pounds, with light brown
hair and hazel eyes. She was last
seen wearing a blue jacket, yellow
blouse, and black and white bell-
bottoms. Persons with any
information are asked to notify
city police.

After seeing my picture in the local paper today, October 15, 1970, I feel confused, fearful and wanted. I don't know if I should continue to allow those few people who are hiding me out to continue to do so. I know if the authorities find out, they could prosecute them for harboring a minor. If Dad and Kathy were to find out, they for sure would have them arrested. I don't want to walk the streets. The police will find me. I don't want to sleep in the park. It's dark and cold there at night. I feel as though I am a fugitive. I decide to accept the help of those who are willing to hide and keep me safe. Although I've shared specifics about Kathy, I never tell anyone about the "special" relationship that Dad and I have. I can't. It is our secret.

A few days have passed. I meet Karen, who works at the local Girls' Club. She is tall; medium built, has blonde hair and seems to genuinely care about me. She asks many questions. I don't hesitate to share my thoughts and feelings about the way Kathy treats me. I don't tell her about the relationship that Dad and I have. After much discussion, she convinces me that we should go to talk with my worker, Diane Meier, at the Welfare Department. This makes sense to me, she knows the family history and maybe now she will do something. I agree to do this, as long as she comes with me.

The following day, when I awaken, I can feel all the muscles in my stomach tightenup. The palms of my hands become moist. I don't have an appetite. I'm nervous and scared. I wonder what will happen later today.

It is mid-afternoon. Karen arrives. It is obvious to her that something is wrong.

She asks, "How are you?"

I look at her and say, "I'm scared."

She assures me, "It will be alright. I will be with you."

We arrive at the Welfare Department. God, I feel sick to my stomach. What if Dad and Kathy are here? What will I do? Karen asks to speak with Diane Meier. She is told that Diane Meier no longer has the case. I feel panic stricken. I want to run out of the building. Before I am able to muster up enough nerve to do so, a man appears. He is tall, with dark hair and a mustache. He eyeballs me and then looking at Karen says, "I am Bob Drake, the caseworker." Karen lets him know that we are here to see Diane Meier. Again, Karen is told that Diane Meier is no longer the worker.

Throughout the next twelve months, I am placed in a number of "temporary" foster homes. Because of my habitual running away, I then spend time at the local detention center. This is of my own doing. I would spend a couple of weeks in a foster home, and then begin to feel guilty after the visits and talks I have with Dad. I then would return home. I was only able to tolerate home life for two, three months, at a time. Then, I was on the run again. Nothing had changed at home. Kathy's temper would flare-up, without warning. I was still taking care of everyone. Dad and I maintained our relationship.

It was in the spring of 1971 that things seemed to shift for me. I was enrolled in a nursing program and worked part-time at a local nursing home on the weekends. It kept me busy, I got paid, and I was away from the house. I didn't feel the need to run away.

Mr. Drake didn't feel that he needed to keep the case open any longer. He felt that both Dad and Kathy were capable of caring for their children. If he "really" knew what went on in this family, he wouldn't be so quick to close the case. Although there were times that I would get upset with Mr. Drake because he would tell me that I was being "manipulative," I liked him. I sensed that he genuinely cared about me.

The fall of 1971 would bring yet more changes. Kathy once again shows her "true colors." She becomes as mean as ever. I have been able to tolerate her behavior for the past few months, but once again, home life has become unbearable. Dad chooses to ignore her. I don't know how he is able to do this. She is so loud and mean. I become more verbal about Kathy when Dad comes to my room at night. This doesn't make a difference. It doesn't seem as though Dad is interested in hearing what I think or feel. I begin to feel that I am his mistress. I feel used. I feel dirty. I feel betrayed. It is then that I realize that things will never change.

I never gave much thought to the fact that my last name isn't the same as Dad's or Junior's. So, one day, I ask Dad why this is. He tells me he was never able to afford to change my last name when my mother died. I don't give much thought to his answer until a few weeks later. It is then that I realize that because my last name is different, I must have another father, someplace, or somewhere. I am determined to find out who he is. I have finally built up enough nerve to ask Dad. The palms of my hands are sweating. I can feel the muscles in my stomach tighten. What will he tell me?

I ask him, " Are you my father?"

He looks at me and says, " You are my special little girl."

I ask, again.

He doesn't answer.

I say, " I don't want to live here. I want to know who my 'real' father is. I know that you aren't my father!"

He stands there not saying a word. He looks sad. He has tears in his eyes.

I say, "If you don't tell me, I will run away and find him myself."

He looks at me and says, " You can call your Aunt Cecilia. She will tell you who your father is."

I look at him and say, " I thought you loved me. You just use me!"

He stands there, pulls a piece of folded paper from his wallet, and hands it to me.

I unfold the piece of paper. It has Aunt Cecilia's name and phone number on it.

He looks at me and says, "I love you."

I look at him and say, " You don't love me! You just use me!"

He doesn't say a word. It's as though he doesn't hear a word that I am saying.

I ask, " How did you get Aunt Cecilia's number?"

He tells me, " When you ran away before."

I let him know that I am going to call her.

He moves toward me. I back away. He reaches for me. I say, " Don't touch me."

He says, " I love you."

I look at him and say, " I love you, too."

I place the piece of paper in my pocket. I feel numb. I feel confused. I don't know what to do. I love Dad. I need him. The piece of paper with Aunt Cecilia's name and number would be tucked away in a safe place for five months. It was then that she and I would have a conversation on the phone. It was then that she and I would formulate a plan to be reunited.

It is mid – October and I am at my wit's end. Once again, I run away. Because many of the neighbors seem to know how cruel and violent Kathy is, it isn't difficult to recruit a few of them to hide me out. For a number of weeks I stay with a family that lives only two doors from the very dwelling that I ran away from. I stay inside all day long, and then sit on the porch or go for a walk in the middle of the night. The neighborhood is quiet and it is safe to surface. My time clock has to be reversed, my days become nights, and my nights become days. Although this is a major adjustment, I don't mind, it is a small price to pay for freedom.

November 8, 1971, would be my last taste of freedom for a while. The home that provided a barrier and protection for me catches on fire. In all the panic and confusion while evacuating the home, a neighbor sees me standing outside. This wasn't a neighbor who was recruited to hide me out. Although the people I am staying with whisk me off to a place that they think will be safe, the local police question them. Before I know what is happening, the police appear.

They tell me I have to come with them. I resist, and tell them that I am not going. Next thing I know, Dad shows up. He looks at me and says, " I'll teach you, they can lock you up." I scream and yell at the police officers and tell them that I am not going back home. The police officers subdue me. I'm handcuffed and taken to the local detention home. I am intimidated, scared and full of fear. I have not hurt anyone. I ran away to be free of them. All of a sudden, I feel as though I have done something wrong.

The next couple of months would be spent at the local detention home. Although it is a locked facility, I don't mind being there. The building is small. It is staffed twenty-four hours a day. Each night, I am locked in my room. This doesn't bother me. I feel safe. I feel cared for. No one yells at me. I don't get hit. I don't have to perform sexual acts for anyone. I don't have to take care of anyone. I just need to be me. Each room has a window. There are nights that I stand at my window, peering out, watching the staff leave. I wish so much that I could go home with one of them.

Every so often I have to appear in Family Court. I am told this is because the Judge has to issue a remand for me to continue to stay at the detention home. I dread those days that I am transported from the facility to Family Court. Walking from the car to the courthouse and then to the courtroom is the worst part. People on the street stare at me and then once I enter the courthouse it seems as though everyone is looking at me. I feel embarrassed. I feel as though I am a criminal.

Prior to appearing in front of the Judge, I, along with others, sit on a hard wooden bench and wait for my case to be called. Sometimes I wait for an hour or longer, and then only to be in the courtroom for less than ten minutes. The Judge addresses the adults and not me. This doesn't make sense to me. Although I am not spoken to, I don't mind. During the ten minutes or so that I am in his courtroom, my knees shake the entire time. The Judge has a deep gruff voice. When he speaks, there is silence in the room. It is obvious that he is in control of what does and doesn't happen in his courtroom.

A few weeks have passed. Today's court appearance would be unlike the others. Today, I witness just how much power and authority the Judge has. Both Dad and Kathy are in the courtroom with me, appearing before the Judge. This is unusual. Kathy never comes to court. As the Judge is verbalizing that he is ordering another remand, Kathy reacts. Loudly and with anger in her voice she says, " You whore. You bitch. They need to lock you up." Next thing I know, she lunges for me. I pull away. The Judge orders the deputy to handcuff her. He holds her in contempt of court. She gets arrested. I can feel my knees shaking. I feel sick to my stomach. I look at the Judge. He says nothing. I look at Dad. He stands in silence. I turn my head to the right and notice a tall, medium built woman standing near the door. Although she is dressed in street clothes, she wears a habit. I wonder who she is. She looks concerned, but doesn't say a word. As I exit the courthouse with the transporter I think to myself, " Yes, she finally got what she deserves! Maybe they will never let her out of jail. I hope not."

Days and weeks pass. I remain at the detention home. Although I've spent Thanksgiving, Christmas and New Years here, I haven't minded. The holidays have been so peaceful. No yelling. No arguments. When someone speaks to me, they do so with respect and gentleness.

Today, I have a visitor. I wonder who it is. I know it can't be Dad. I refuse to see him. This person comes to my room. The door is left unlocked and open. She introduces herself as Sister Connie. I recognize her. She is the person who was standing near the door in the courtroom the day Kathy was arrested. She tells me that she is the Family Court Chaplin. I have no idea what a Family Court Chaplin is. I feel stupid and too embarrassed to ask her to explain. So, I sit in silence. She reaches into her pocket and pulls out a Clarke Bar and offers it to me. I say, "No, thank you." She makes many attempts to engage in conversation with me. But, I just listen. She then asks, "Do you want to go home?" I don't hesitate to answer. I say, "I don't and won't go home." She asks why? I repeat, " I don't and won't go home." Sister Connie visits me quite often during my stay at the detention home. She becomes a permanent fixture in the courtroom when I appear before the Judge.

Throughout my stay at the detention home I make friends with other kids who are being detained. I feel a close bond to them. We have something in common. We have been remanded to the facility through Family Court. Although there are rules at the detention home the staff at times become very lenient. Tonight after showers are taken, a few of us decide to have a powder fight. It wasn't planned. It just happened. We childishly begin to throw baby powder at one another. Things get out of hand and before you know it, baby powder is all over the place. Ms. Tepper, who is working this evening, walks into the bathroom area. None of us say a word. We stand in silence. She looks at us and says, "What are you doing?" Before any of us have a chance to utter a word, she starts laughing. After she composes herself, she tells us, "Okay, you've had your fun, now it is time to clean it up." We do this without hesitation. Laughter fills the room.

Although I have a common bond with the other kids at the detention home I, unlike them, have no desire to go home. I develop relationships with other detainees and they leave. Some go home and some are sent to institutions. I realize that I can't stay here forever. Although the staff at the detention home remains the same, I know that I need to come up with a plan. If I don't make a plan, someone will make one for me. I don't want to be sent to an institution. I don't want to go home. I begin to formulate a plan. I know if I ask to see Dad, he will come to see me. I also know that if I tell him I want to come home, I will be able to go home. The goal then becomes coming up with a plan before a plan is made for me.

I decide it would be best for me to go home. Although I don't want to live at home I know that going home will enable me to formulate a plan. I've been home now for a couple of weeks. Remember Aunt Cecilia. Well, she and I have connected. I kept that piece of paper with her phone number tucked away in a safe place all these months. I've spoken to her a few times. I ask that she not tell Dad that I call. She agrees not to tell him. Because she lives in San Francisco, California and I have no money, I call collect. She never refuses to accept the call. The first conversation we have, I feel so warm and fuzzy inside. I remember back to when I was a young child. She comforted me. She made me feel safe. I felt loved and cared for. All those feelings resurface. I tell her that I don't want to live here. I tell her that I know Dad is not my real father. I tell her how mean Kathy is. I tell her that Dad does things to me. I ask if I

8

can come live with her. Without hesitation she tells me I can. It's as if she knows something that I don't.

A few days have passed. Aunt Cecilia has made arrangements for me to take a Greyhound bus to San Francisco where she and I will be reunited. I tell no one. I don't want anyone to know where I am. As I make my way to the bus station I don't fill my head with thoughts of Dad, Kathy, Michael, Joey or Junior. I fill my head with thoughts of Aunt Cecilia. I know she loves me. I know she cares about me. I know she won't hurt me. I know that she will protect me

Chapter Two

My Roots

My journey to San Francisco would bring with it many discoveries. I would be reunited with Aunt Cecilia. She would once again bring joy and happiness back into my life. It would also be a time of much confusion, pain and turmoil. In asking questions, I would discover my roots.

The long ride from Syracuse has finally ended. I arrive at the bus station in San Francisco. As the bus comes to a stop, I look out the window and scan the many faces. Aunt Cecilia sounded the same on the phone as I remembered her when I was a young child. It's been so many years since I last saw her. I have no idea what she looks like. I sit on my seat and wait for others to exit. I'm the last one on the bus. I get up slowly and walk down the aisle, hoping that Aunt Cecilia will see me. As my feet hit the hard concrete pavement, I wonder to myself, "What does she look like? Will she recognize me?" Before another thought enters my head, I hear my name. I turn my head and look in the direction that the voice is coming from. Sure enough, it is Aunt Cecilia. She approaches me with open arms. She has the same warm smile that I remember as a child. She embraces me. God, it feels so good to be in her arms. We stand, holding onto one another for what seems to be a long time. She cries. I cry. She tells me that she has missed me. Those words warm my heart. As we exit the bus station we hold onto one another's hand. I feel safe. I feel loved.

During the drive from the bus station to Aunt Cecilia's apartment in Daley City, she tells me that I have two nieces and one nephew. I hadn't known this. She tells me that they are excited to meet me. She goes on to tell me that she divorced my uncle a couple of years ago, and that she is a single parent. She doesn't offer any other information. I don't know what to say. I sit in silence. I think to myself, "I hope they like me."

A month has passed since I've been living with Aunt Cecilia. It seemed to pass so quickly. The atmosphere is so relaxed. There is no yelling. No screaming. No one hits me. No one asks me to do sexual acts. Although Aunt Cecilia has rules, I don't mind. She is not demanding. She is fair. When she asks me to do something she does so with kindness in her voice. Although my nieces and nephew are younger than I, I like them. They are well behaved, polite and have good manners. It is clear to me that they love and respect their mother. It is also clear that they like me. I like being called "Aunt Cathy." I feel right at home.

A few weeks have passed. I begin to wonder how I can be Aunt Cecilia's niece and also be the aunt of her children. I thought her children were supposed to be my cousins? So, one day I ask her why this is. I'm told that my biological father is my grandfather, which would make Aunt Cecilia my half-sister and aunt, which then makes me the aunt of her children. I have a hard time taking in all that has just been shared. I thought Dad was my father. I feel so confused. Although my last name is different from his, he has always taken care of me. My body begins to feel numb. I don't ask for more information.

I have slept restlessly the past few nights. I lay awake at night thinking about my grandfather. I think about Dad. I think about my Mom. I think about Aunt Cecilia. I then remember back to when I was very young, when Aunt Cecilia watched both Junior and I while Dad worked. Although I have many cherished memories of those days spent with Aunt Cecilia, I also remember when Dad and Aunt Cecilia would spend time in her bedroom while Junior and I would play in the front room. I now know that they must have been sleeping with one another. This must be why my uncle got so upset. This must be why he was waving the knife in the air. This must be why he told Dad, "Get out, or I will kill you." I didn't understand then, but I understand now. So many questions enter my head, as I lay awake at night. How could Dad after knowing that my grandfather was my biological father do the same to me that was done to my Mom? Although we didn't have a child, he still sexually abused me for all those years. How dare him tell me that I looked like my Mom? How dare him tell me that I was "special?" How dare my grandfather take advantage of my mother? How dare them! How dare them all!

A number of days have passed. I'm consumed with thoughts and feelings. The information that Aunt Cecilia shared with me doesn't seem to bother her. Her mood doesn't change. She doesn't treat me differently. It seems as though she has forgotten what she told me. I approach her and let her know that I want to speak with my grandfather. The look on her face is one of surprise. As I look into her hazel eyes, I see compassion. It's as though she knows what thoughts and feelings are running through my body without words being spoken. She asks, "Are you sure?" I say, "Yes."

The time has come to make the call. God, I'm so nervous. What will I say? What will he say? What will he sound like? Aunt Cecilia dials his number. I sit at the kitchen table across from her. I feel my stomach muscles tighten up. The palms of my hands are moist. I feel sick to my stomach. He answers. Aunt Cecilia says, "Hi Dad, this is Cecilia." I feel like throwing up. She called him Dad. Am I supposed to call him Dad? No, I won't call him Dad. Although a few seconds pass, it feels like minutes. Aunt Cecilia looks at me and says, "Here you go." I reach for the phone. I put it to my ear. I say, "Hello." He says, "Cathy, this is your Dad." He has excitement in his voice. I want to scream. I want to yell. Instead, I say nothing. A few seconds pass. He says, " I love you." My body begins to feel numb. He sounds old. He sounds frail. I pull the phone away from my ear and hand it to Aunt Cecilia. I tell her, "I don't want to talk to him." I get up and walk away from the table. He and Aunt Cecilia

13

converse for a few minutes. I am filled with anger. I am filled with disappointment. I'm so confused. How can he tell me that he loves me after what he did? Why does my "real" father have to be my grandfather?

I try to make sense of all the information that has been given to me. The more I try, the angrier I get. The more I try, the more confused I get. Although I know that Aunt Cecilia loves and cares about me, I have a difficult time with her being my aunt and also being my half-sister. I asked questions because I wanted to discover my roots. I wanted to find out who my "real father" was. Now that I have those answers, I'm not so sure that I want to know.

A few weeks have passed. My restless sleeping patterns have continued. I'm not sure if Aunt Cecilia is aware that I am not sleeping at night. Although I have never had a big appetite, I notice that food hasn't been very appealing to me. I find myself eating at meals because I have to, not because I want to. Aunt Cecilia hasn't mentioned anything about the phone call. I've not said anything to her. I just want to forget about it. I begin to feel like I don't belong with Aunt Cecilia. I'm not sure where I belong. I begin to miss Dad. Although he's not my "real father," he took care of me all those years. I call Dad at work one afternoon when Aunt Cecilia is out doing errands. I tell him that I will be flying home in a couple of days and will call him when I arrive. He doesn't ask any specific questions and I don't offer any information. In reality, I know that I won't be flying home. I haven't a penny to my name. What I decide to do is to get to the Golden Gate Bridge and then hitchhike back home. Although I've never hitch hiked before, I've seen people do it on television. I'm sure I'll get plenty of rides; people will stop to pick me up.

The following day I go to Aunt Cecilia and tell her that I am leaving. I tell her that I can't stay with her. I tell her that I have to go back home, to my Dad. I let her know that I love her. She sits at the table and looks at me. I look into her eyes and see that they are filling with tears. I feel badly, but know that it is time for me to leave. She asks me to stay. I tell her that I can't. She says, " I am sorry." Although she doesn't elaborate about why she is sorry, I know why. She feels bad because I now know who my "real" father is.

14

I have so many mixed emotions. I feel sad. I feel angry. I feel used. I feel abused. I feel lied to. And yet, I feel loved. Aunt Cecilia has let me live with her these past three months. She took care of me when I was younger. She has never been mean to me. I know that she loves me. Why did she sleep with Dad when I was younger? I don't understand! Why does "our" biological father have to be the same person? Why? Why? Why? Instead of continuing to ask myself why and not being able to come up with an answer, I begin my journey back to Syracuse. Dad knows that I am coming. Though he's not my "real father," I know that he loves me.

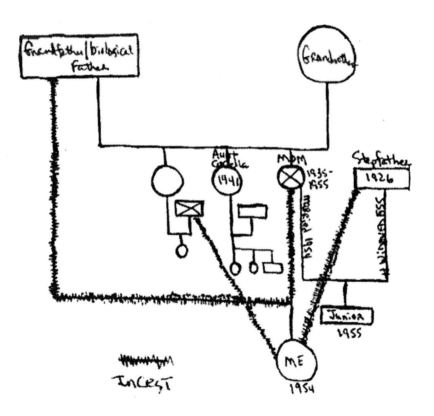

Although my stay with Aunt Cecilia was short lived, I once again felt the joy and happiness that I felt as a child being with her.

Her kindness, gentle ways, honesty and sincerity would forever be remembered and cherished. Although at the time I was unable to see the gift of the discovery of my roots, I am so thankful that she had the courage to share that information with me. In doing so, she would bring clarity and closure to a part of my life; this would have a profound effect on me.

Chapter Three

The Journey Home

My hitchhiking experience from California to New York would bring with it more lessons. I discover that it is illegal to hitchhike in La Porte, Indiana. I first-handedly encounter a ten-day stay at the local jail. This experience is frightening and humiliating. My faith grows deeper. My determination to survive each day grows stronger.

I'm standing in a room at the police station waiting for the officer to return. I gave him Dad's phone number at work. He has gone to call him. I let the officer know that Dad is aware that I was returning home. What I didn't tell him is that I told Dad that I was flying home. The room is big. It has a large table with chairs situated around it. It looks as though meetings are held here. Seconds turn into minutes. I begin to wonder what is taking the officer so long. I hope Dad is at work.

The door opens. The officer walks in the room. He has a female officer with him. I ask anxiously, " Did you talk to my Dad? " He tells me, " I did." I say, " Good, now I can leave." He looks at me and says, " No, you can't leave." I stand in silence for a few moments. I can't believe what I have just heard. What does he mean? Who does he think he is? He breaks the silence and says; "Your father told me that there is an active warrant for you." What does he mean a warrant? I've done nothing wrong. How can this be? As I stand in silence, the officer goes on to say, " Your father filed a P.I.N.S. (Person In Need of Supervision)." I think to myself, "What the hell is that?" The officer goes on to say, "You will be detained here until the Probation Department can arrange for you to be extradited." What does extradited mean? What have I done wrong? I begin to cry. I tell the officer that I want to go home. He tells me, " You will be able to go home." I ask, "When?" He tells me, "When the arrangements are made." He goes on to tell me that they do not have any detention homes and that I will have to stay here at the jail. I ask, " For how long?" He tells me I will have to stay here for about a week. I say, " I've never been in a jail before." He assures me that I will be fine. He introduces me to the female officer and lets me know that she will take care of me. He then politely excuses himself and leaves the room.

The female officer lets me know that I need to strip. She instructs me to take all my clothing off. I stand in silence. I don't make eye contact with her. I stare down at the floor. My body feels frozen. I don't want to take my clothes off. She lets me know that it is procedure. She needs to make sure that I don't have a weapon or drugs. She goes on to say, " Once you take your clothes off, I'll give them back to you." I slowly lift my head. I make eye contact with her. As I disrobe, I hand my clothing to her. I have not taken a shower in days. My clothing is dirty and smells. I'm embarrassed. As quickly as I hand each piece of my clothing to her, she searches it and gives it back to me. Although my clothes are smelly and dirty, I don't waste any time putting them back on.

As the female officer leads me down the long narrow hall to where I will be confined for the next ten days, my stomach muscles begin to tighten. I feel nauseous. I don't want to be here. I have not done anything wrong. I feel scared. I want to run, but I have no place to run to. We turn a corner. I see a large steel door. She inserts her key and pulls it open. To my surprise what I then see is yet another door, but instead of being solid, I see steel bars. She places her key in the hole and swings the door open. She instructs me to follow her.

As we enter she closes the cell door. The walls to this large confined area are solid. Although there are no windows, the room is well lighted by an overhead light. To the right I see a toilet and sink. No door. No shower or tub. I see three females huddled in the corner. The officer lets me know that I will be sharing the cell with them. They look older than I. They say nothing to me. I can hear them whispering. I wonder if they are talking about me. The officer lets me know that I can sleep on one of the mats at night. The mats are blue and about three inches thick. She goes on to tell me that meals are served through the opening in the cell door three times a day. She wishes me well and then leaves. I pull one of the mats out and sit on it. The three women are still huddled in the corner. I wonder why they are in jail. I wonder if I'm going to be safe.

A few days have passed. Although I share the cell with three other women, we don't become friends. They keep their distance. On the second night we engage in conversation. Each of us shares why we are in jail. I tell them that I was returning home and got arrested for hitchhiking. They look at each other and then look at me. It seems as though they are holding back their laughter. I don't see the humor in what I have shared. I don't see what is so funny. I say nothing. I sit and listen. They tell me that they are in jail for prostitution. I have no idea what prostitution is. I don't bother to ask. I don't want them to think that I am stupid.

A few more days pass. The women tell me that today they will go to court and be released. They seem happy. They seem excited. I am relieved and yet saddened. Although I don't feel close to these women, I realize that once they leave, I will be left alone in this dreary, confined room. I hear the key turn in the cell door. The guard comes for them. Before exiting the room, one of the women walks over to me. She has something in her hand. She hands me a bible. She looks at me and says, "Good luck." I say nothing. She turns and walks a short distance behind the others. The cell door closes. I hear the guard turn the key. The room is silent. I clutch the bible to my chest.

In the long days that follow I find myself not looking at the walls or listening for the turning of the guard's key, but I become absorbed with the phrases and short stories in the bible. Although I have always prayed and asked for God's help, I never read the bible. It was always just this book that had words written in it. When I'm not reading my head becomes filled with thoughts and feelings. Each day I become angrier and angrier with Dad. He didn't have to tell the officer that there was a warrant. He could have told the officer to let me go. Why didn't he do this? Why didn't he ask to speak with me? He must be mad at me. It is then that I realize that he has nothing to be mad at me about. I am the one who has many reasons to be mad at him. He told me that he loved me. He told me that I was "special." He used me! He did the very thing to me that my biological father did to my mother. The only difference is I didn't get pregnant. Although I didn't understand at a very young age that he was having an affair with Aunt Cecilia, I now know. How could he do this? Why did he do this? I fear that if I tell anyone about the relationship that he had with her that he will go to jail. I don't want him to go to jail. I just don't want him to touch me. I also know that if I do go home, things won't change. He will sneak around and we will continue to have our " secret affair." I don't want this! I won't go home!

At times I feel confused. At times I feel panic stricken. At times I feel angry with God. If I don't go home where will I stay? How will I eat? Where will I get a job? I'm not able to keep the tears from flowing. I sit on the mat and cry. I rock back and forth. I ask God to help me. It is in those moments that I read and pray. I look for answers, but don't find them. Although answers don't come, I begin to feel calmness within me. I don't know what to think of it. I have not felt this way before. A little voice in my head says, "It will be okay." I don't question the voice or try to figure it out. I just let it be. What I would come to realize is that when I read and pray, I don't feel alone.

The day has arrived for me to leave. I am told that all the paperwork and arrangements for me to be extradited have been completed. As I sit on the mat waiting patiently in this room that I have been confined to for ten days, I reflect upon the time that has been spent here. Initially, I felt frightened and humiliated, but as time passed this changed for me. My confinement became my safe haven; a time for me to think, a time for me to feel, a time for me to rediscover my faith, and a time for me to become more determined to face each day. As I sit holding the bible that was given to me close to my chest, I feel so thankful.

I hear the key turn in the cell door. It must be the guard coming for me. I look. The door swings open. She looks at me with a smile on her face and says, " It is time to leave." I stand and walk towards her. I realize that I have the bible that was given to me. It doesn't feel right for me to take it. I turn and walk back to the mat that I have sat and slept on for these past ten days. I bend down and place the bible on the mat. I turn and walk towards the door. I now know that there isn't anything that I can't do. I think to myself, " Thank you, God!"

Chapter Four

Set Free

My return to Syracuse, New York would bring with it many gifts. I would once again spend a short period of time at the detention home. I would once again appear in front of the Family Court Judge. The time spent at the detention home was good for me. I was safe. I was able to sort out my thoughts and feelings. I begin to give myself permission to use my voice, rather than keeping thoughts and feelings to myself. Appearing in front of the Family Court Judge is scary. His decision with a stern warning to never return to his courtroom again would change my life. I would become an emancipated minor. I would be "Set Free."

I have arrived in Syracuse. As I exit the plane, two detectives greet me. They let me know that they will be taking me to the detention home. I don't resist. I don't ask any questions. I go with them. The drive from the airport to the detention home allows me to think. I reflect upon my last stay at the detention home. All the staff was nice to me. I had fun there. I felt safe. Although, once again, I will be detained in a locked building, this doesn't bother me. I know that I won't be locked in a cell. I know that the staff cares about me. I wonder if they know that I am coming? They must.

A few days have passed. I have settled into the daily routine here at the detention home. It sure feels good to be back here. Staff tells me that I seem different. I am told that I smile more. I am told that I look happier and at peace with myself. I share with the staff what it was like for me to be locked up in a cell for ten days. I tell them how lonely I was. I tell them how sad I felt. I tell them that I felt like a prisoner. I want so badly to share about what I discovered about my "family roots," but I can't. I don't want anyone to get into trouble. I don't want Dad to go to jail. I don't want anyone to know that my grandfather is my biological father. I say nothing about my family discoveries.

The day has come to appear in Family Court. As I walk from the vehicle to the courthouse, unlike other times, I don't feel embarrassed. Instead of looking down at my feet, I look straight ahead. Although people in the halls of the courthouse look at me, it doesn't bother me like it did in the past. I know that I have done nothing wrong. The past couple of days I have rehearsed this day in my head. I know that I will see Dad. I'm not sure if Kathy will be in court. I will tell the Judge that I don't want to go home. I will tell the Judge that I want to be on my own. I will tell Dad that I know the truth. I will tell him I know who my "real" father is. I will tell him that I never want to see him again.

As I sit on the hard wooden bench in the waiting area outside the courtroom, I keep my eyes fixed on the doorway. I am looking for Dad. I wonder where he is? A familiar looking person enters the room. It is not Dad, but Sister Connie. She walks towards me with a smile on her face. She looks happy to see me. She asks, "How are you?" I say, "fine." She sits on the bench next to me. I look at her and say, " I'm not going home. I will never go back there." She asks, "Where will you go? You have no one to take care of you." I tell her, "I don't need anyone to take care of me. I can take care of myself." She lets me know that the Judge is not going to be happy that I am once again appearing in front of him. I let her know that I don't care what the Judge thinks. I tell her that I am going to let the Judge know that I am not going home. I tell her that I am going to ask the Judge to let me be on my own. Before I have a chance to utter another word she says, " But Cathy, the streets are not safe and terrible things

24

happen to people." As I sit and listen to her words I think to myself, "Terrible things have already happened to me. If you only knew what I have endured."

Dad walks into the waiting area. Good, I don't see Kathy with him. He walks towards me. I don't get up to give him a hug: instead, I just look up at him. Both he and Sister Connie exchange hellos. I look at him and say, " I'm not coming home." With assertiveness in his voice he says, "We'll see what the Judge has to say about that. Cathy, I love you and want you to come home." His intimidation tactics no longer have a hold on me. I now know that when he says, "I love you," what he really means is that he likes what I do for him sexually. I become angry. I stand up and look into his eyes. I tell him, " I am not coming home. I don't want to ever see you again. I know the truth. Aunt Cecelia told me. Just leave me alone!" He stands in silence. I notice that his eyes are filling with tears. This doesn't bother me. I don't care how he feels.

The court attendant summons us to the courtroom. I stand. My knees wobble. My stomach muscles begin to tighten. As I enter the courtroom it takes all the strength within me to compose myself. I am scared. Unlike other times I don't stand and look down at the courtroom floor, but keep my eyes fixed on the Judge. In the past the Judge has only spoken to the adults. I always felt that I was being talked about rather than spoken too. Today is different. The Judge looks at me and says, " You can't stay put. I am remanding you back to the detention home." Before he is able to utter another word I say, " I don't want to go home. I want to be on my own." For a few seconds there is silence in the courtroom. It's as though no one expected me to say a word. The silence is broken by the Judge's deep stern voice. He looks at me and says, " You will go back to the detention home and I will see you on the next court date." As I exit the courtroom and make my way to the waiting area, I look at Dad. He looks at me. He says, " Cathy, please come home." I look into his deep brown eyes. They are filled with sadness. His words sound sincere. I am consumed with my own thoughts and feelings. I say, "Good bye" and walk away.

The weeks that would follow at the detention home are a welcome respite. Although I am being detained, I don't mind. My basic needs are being met. I am able to sort out my thoughts and feelings. Throughout this process there are moments when things become cloudy. In those moments I find myself not focusing on my own feelings and needs, but the feelings and needs that Dad might have. The thought of being back home again quickly awakens me. I come to my senses. I have flashbacks of spending time with Dad at night, remembering how painful and uncomfortable those times were, remembering his words "I love you" and realizing that he only loved what I did for him. The question keeps popping up in my head. Why did he do the very same thing to me that was done to my mother? I search myself and can't find an answer. It was wrong. It was unfair. It is unforgivable. It is at this point that I realize that none of it was my fault. I am a kid. He is the adult. It becomes crystal clear to me why I can't and won't go back home.

Sister Connie visits me quite often. I look forward to her coming and enjoy the time we spend with one another. Although at times she becomes somewhat "preachy," I don't mind. I sit and listen to her words. She talks about how God loves me. She tells me that God will protect me. There is a part of me that knows this to be true, but there is also a part of me that questions why HE allowed all those things to happen to me. I don't voice the thoughts that enter my head. I can't. My secret has to remain a secret. I wonder if she feels sorry for me. Ah, it doesn't really matter. I like spending time with her. I like her. All the other kids who are being detained have visitors. I don't. I refuse to see Dad. She and the staff ask why I don't want to see him. I just say, " I don't want to see him." I don't elaborate. I don't offer any information. I am not pressured to talk about why I don't want to see him. My request is honored and accepted. For the first time in my life I feel like I am being listened to. I feel cared about.

The day has arrived for me to return to court. Other times, I have appeared in front of the Judge in the morning. Today, I will stand before the Judge in the afternoon. A couple of days ago while Sister Connie and I were visiting she told me that she spoke to the Judge. I ask her why. She tells me that she spoke to him because she cares about me. She went on to say that the Judge felt that I should be sent away to an institution. I looked at her and said, "I didn't do anything wrong. If he sends me away, I will run." I tell her with determination in my voice, "I can take care of myself. I don't need or want anyone to take care of me." She lets me know that there is a possibility that the Judge will allow me to be on my own. This morning, as I think about standing before the Judge this afternoon, I remember her words. Instead of becoming anxious and filling my head with thoughts of an institution. I think about how it will feel to never be sexually abused again. I think about how it will feel to never be beaten again. I think about how it will feel to never be emotionally abused again. I think about how it will feel to never have to go home again. I fill my head with thoughts of being set free.

I am told that the transporter has arrived to take me to court. As I make my way to the front of the building with the paper bag that is filled with all my possessions I think to myself, " If I don't return, I will miss this place." Before exiting the building I am wished "good luck" by the staff who are working. I look at each of them and let them know that they will be missed. I say, " Maybe one day I will come back to volunteer." It's as though we all know that a decision will be made. What that decision will be is yet to be known.

Although the transporter attempts to engage me in conversation, I don't say much. I am consumed with thoughts and feelings. I wonder if Kathy will be in court. I hope not. If she is, I will ignore her. I don't want to hear her mean words. I don't want to be embarrassed again by her actions. What if the Judge sends me to an institution? No, that can't happen. I won't go! I wonder what Dad will say to me. I won't listen to his words. His words are just words. They no longer have meaning to me. I wonder if Sister Connie will be in court. I hope so.

The car stops. I notice we are parked in front of the courthouse. Unlike other times, the drive from the detention home to court seems short. As I exit the car, I say a silent prayer. I ask God to PLEASE help me. I feel the sidewalk beneath my feet. I take a deep breath. My stomach muscles aren't tight. The palms of my hands aren't moist. I feel calmness throughout my body. I walk from the car to the courthouse. I am centered and focused.

As I enter the waiting area to the courtroom, I scan for familiar faces. I see Dad. It doesn't look like Kathy is with him. He looks at me. I look at him. He walks toward me. I can feel my stomach muscles begin to tighten. His body looks rigid. He looks worried. He stands in front of me and says, " I want you to come home!" I look at him. I'm scared. I'm nervous. A few seconds pass. I search for words. I look at him and say, " I'm not coming home! I will never come home. You are not going to get what you want!" Before any other words are spoken, Sister Connie appears. Thank God! She walks towards us. As she is greeting us, she positions her body between Dad and I. The moment becomes less intense. My stomach isn't as tight. I feel a wave of calmness fill my body. Dad looks at her and says, " I want her home!" Sister Connie looks at him with self-assurance in her voice and says, " The Judge will make that decision." Dad says, " She is only a kid. She can't take care of herself." I think to myself, "What does he mean, I can't take care of myself? How dare he say this? He only cares about what I can do for him!" I'm not able to contain my thoughts in my head. I look at both of them and say, " I am not coming home! You can't make me come home! You don't love me! You just use me!" Neither of them says a word. It's as though they are surprised that I spoke.

The court attendant summons us to the courtroom. As I walk from the waiting area to the courtroom, where my fate will be decided, I ask God to not let the Judge send me home. As I stand before the bench, I look up at the Judge. He is a big man. He looks so powerful sitting in his chair with his black cape on. He looks gruff. I wait patiently for his words to be spoken. He addresses all the adults standing before him and then addresses me. With his deep stern voice he tells me that he is going to declare me an emancipated minor. I have no idea what he means. What is an emancipated minor? Does this mean that I don't have to go home? Does this mean that he isn't going to send me to an institution? Before another thought enters my head the Judge looks at me and says with a stern voice, " If you ever enter my courtroom again, you better bring your toothbrush." My eyes lock with his. Before I am able to utter a word,

Dad speaks up. He says, " She is too young to be on her own." The Judge responds by saying, " This is my courtroom and this is my ruling." The Judge looks at me and says, " Cathy, you are free to go." I don't know what to say. I look at the Judge. I want to say, "thank you" but I'm not able to speak. The Judge says, " Next case." One by one we walk out of the courtroom. Dad exits the courtroom first. As Sister Connie and I are standing in the waiting area, Dad turns his head and looks at me. He looks angry. He looks sad. He looks defeated. I look at him and say, " Good bye." He walks away. My total being feels relieved. I feel as though I have been set free.

At the time of the writing of this book Sister Connie still remains a part of my life. Her perseverance in advocating for me thirty-three years ago and her diligent effort truly made a difference in my fate.

Chapter Five

Discovering My Limits

Becoming an emancipated minor in the spring of 1971 afforded me the opportunity to make my own decisions. I decided to live with a family who once lived in my old neighborhood. The time spent living with this family would be short lived. I would get a taste of what it is like to live with an active alcoholic. For the first time in my life, I would share the details of the relationship I had with my stepfather. In doing so, I would pay dearly. I would feel betrayed, angry and hurt.

I've lived with Barbara and her family for a couple of weeks. Although I sleep on the sofa, I don't mind. The apartment is clean, warm and dry. I'm not living on the streets. I feel safe. I have not been able to find a job. My skills are limited. I am told that I can apply for public assistance, but I don't. It has been my experience throughout my life that if someone gives something to me, I, then, have to give something in return. I am no longer willing to allow this to happen. Although I am not working, this doesn't seem to bother Barbara. I help out around the apartment, doing dishes, tidying up and sometimes fixing dinner for everyone. Although my skills in the area of cooking are not great, no one ever complains. Barbara usually sleeps until noon. She is up most of the night drinking.

A few more weeks have passed. One night while Barbara is sitting at the kitchen table drinking, she asks me, " Did you sleep with your father?" God, how I have yearned, for so many years, for someone to ask me this very question. I look at her and say, "Yes." I wait patiently for her to ask me another question. Instead, she sits at the table and continues to drink. It's as though she has forgotten that I am in the same room. A few more minutes pass. Rather than standing there watching her drink, I walk into the front room. I sit on the sofa. I wonder to myself, " Did I say something wrong? Did I do something wrong?"

A couple of days have passed. Tonight, unlike other nights when Barbara is drinking, she becomes very loud and argumentative. I have not seen her like this before. She walks into the front room. I'm sitting on the sofa. She looks at me with anger in her voice and says, " You whore." I don't know what to say. I don't know what to do. I know she is drunk. I try to ignore her. She becomes louder. She stands in front of me and yells out, " You fuck your father." I look at her. I can't believe the words I hear coming from her mouth. Again, I try to ignore her. She continues to yell out those words, repeatedly. I tell her, " Shut up!" She doesn't listen. She is standing in front of me. I push her out of the way and walk into the kitchen. I reach for the phone and dial Sister Connie's phone number. It's late. I hope she is still up. She answers. I say, "Sister Connie" and begin to sob. She can hear Barbara screaming at me in the background. She asks, "What is wrong?" I am able to mutter the words, " Please, come and get me!" She says, "I'll be right there." I grab a paper bag and throw the few pieces of clothing I have in it. Barbara continues to walk about the apartment screaming. I decide not to wait for Sister Connie inside the apartment. I can't stand the screaming. Before exiting the apartment, I look at Barbara. She looks out of control. She looks so mean. She looks angry. Without saying good-bye, I open the door and leave. As I stand on the porch waiting for Sister Connie, I hear her yelling out those unkind words. I am so angry. I feel so hurt. I feel betrayed. I trusted her.

It would be a number of years before I would come to terms with the feelings that I held deep inside regarding this incident. I would come to realize through therapy and relationships with other people that Barbara's reaction and unkind words were not a reflection of who I was, but a reflection of her own unresolved issues. I would also come to realize that during that period of time in my life, I consciously made a decision as to what I would and would not tolerate. Being blamed by anyone for having an incestuous relationship with my stepfather was not acceptable. Although my stay with Barbara and her family was short lived, I was grateful to have a place to stay. I was grateful not to be living on the streets. I was grateful for the discovery of what I was and was not willing to tolerate.

Chapter Six

Unconditional Love

Shortly after leaving Barbara and her family I move to the Young Women's Christian Association. Within this organization is a program called the Special Residence Project. It is here that I begin to let down my guard and allow others to care about me. It is here that I am introduced to the concept of unconditional love.

I have my own room. It consists of a bed and dresser. There are no pictures or decorations on the walls. In fact, the room doesn't look like it has been painted for quite some time. It is depressing. I tell myself, " I will fix it up. I'll buy some posters and put them on the walls. I'll make it cheerful. I'll brighten it up." Although I have my own room, the bathroom, kitchen and television area are treated as common space. At any given time other people occupy these spaces. I like this. It forces me to interact with others, rather than isolate myself in my room.

A few months pass. Some of the folks who are staying here are going to college. Others have either relocated or become estranged from their family. I begin to realize that I have much more in common with the other residents than not. Initially, I feel somewhat intimidated by those who are going to college. Although I am verbal, my vocabulary doesn't consist of sophisticated words. I didn't graduate from high school. I don't have the big words to use. I can't relate to what it is like to travel to and from a campus daily. I certainly can relate to what it is like to be estranged from one's family. Although others share their stories with me, I share very little about my family. I can't take the risk of someone blaming me. I remain guarded. This doesn't seem to matter to my newfound friends.

As time passes I begin to realize that each of them care about me simply because I am me. This is a new concept for me. Any relationships that I have had in the past entailed giving something in return. More times than not, this would mean sexual favors. Over time, I begin to share bits and pieces about myself. I slowly let down my guard. It feels good. It feels right to share with others. It's nice to have someone listen. Over time I begin to feel more self-assured. My self-image improves. I move towards seeing myself as a worthy person rather than one who is unworthy. I begin to gain more respect for myself. I begin to embrace life rather than exist from day to day. In taking the risk to allow myself to form relationships with others and to allow others to care about me, I begin to blossom.

Shortly after I move to the Young Women's Christian Association I develop a relationship with the Residential Director, Judy. I initially met her during the interview process. The only way I could move into the program was to be interviewed by her. It seemed that the program was tailored for me. The two main requirements were to check-in on a weekly basis with the residential director and to pay my rent on time. I didn't feel that either of these requirements was unreasonable. I was also aware that the program offered counseling and referrals. I didn't need or want anyone to try to fix the pain that I felt within me. All I needed was a safe place to stay. Judy is tall, slender, and has long dark flowing hair. Her eyes are filled with compassion. I sense that she is an insightful person. It was obvious to me at the onset of our initial contact that she genuinely cares about others. Her smile is radiant and puts one at ease. I've never seen anyone as beautiful as she. I was so nervous the day of and prior to our initial contact. Having no place to stay, I knew that this interview was important. I thought for sure that she wouldn't like me. I thought for sure that I would be told that I couldn't move in.

Although my anxiety level was high, I composed myself. I couldn't let her know how desperate I was. The interview went fine. I could move in immediately. Without knowing it at the time she would become an important person in my life.

I am faced with a dilemma. Do I take the risk of becoming vulnerable? Do I allow Judy to become a part of my world? Through time my relationship with Judy would flourish. Although I am cautious and guarded, she is able to break down those barriers with time and perseverance. I am resistant. I am afraid to allow her to get close to me emotionally. My heart is heavily burdened with not only the loss of my siblings, but also the loss of my stepfather. There are moments that my head becomes flooded with emotions. I miss not having a family. I miss my stepfather. As quickly as those emotions surface the memories of how terrible it was for me all those years emerge. I would once again be reminded through memories that my decision to sever those ties was a healthy one.

Throughout the spring, summer and fall of 1971, I would become acquainted with the term unconditional love. Although I see Judy on a daily basis, throughout the week, I also begin to spend time with her and her husband, Sam, outside her work setting. He is tall. Handsome. He is a person of medium build. He has a good sense of humor. When the three of us are together there is no lull in conversation. We joke, laugh and talk about things that we agree on and those things that we don't agree on. I feel no pressure from either of them to give or say anything that doesn't feel natural or good for me. They accept me for who I am. Although I have let my guard down, I await that moment when they will show disapproval. I anticipate the moment when they too will disappear from my life. It would be in the fall that my thinking would shift. I begin to feel warm and fuzzy inside when I am with or think about Sam and Judy. I no longer think about or dwell on the moment that either one of them will disappear from my life. Our relationship feels good. It feels right. I know beyond a doubt that they are just as much a part of my life as I am theirs. I no longer have the need to remain guarded. I feel cared about. I feel loved.

I have no job skills to speak of. I am very neat and well organized. I know that I want to work with people, but am not at all sure how that is going to happen. I feel as though I am in limbo. My rent bill is adding up. I begin to get nervous. I begin to fear that I am going to be asked to leave because I am unable to pay my rent. I think about applying for public assistance. No, I can't. No, I won't. If I apply for public assistance then I owe someone something. I don't want to owe anyone anything. My anxiety increases. Judy senses this. She assures me that I won't get kicked out. She and I begin to explore alternatives, other than public assistance. Within a few days my anxiety would be lifted. The burden of worrying about how I was going to eat and pay my rent would no longer be a concern. Sam asked if I would clean his law office on a weekly basis. Judy asked if I would clean their home on a weekly basis. A few of their friends contacted me and asked if I would be willing to clean their homes weekly. I didn't hesitate to say "yes" to any of them. I would have enough money to pay my rent. I would have enough money to eat. Although I didn't need to burden myself with how I was going to pay my rent or eat, I continue to look for a job. A few months pass. I am offered a full-time job at a local Day Care Center. I accept the position as a Day Care Center Aide. I will be paid an hourly wage. I have health insurance. I can accumulate vacation and sick days. I am excited. I am proud. Life is good.

I rely on the local bus system. It's reliable and my only means of transportation. Often times when I am on the bus I think about how nice it would be to have my own vehicle. Although I know that I can't afford a car, I decide to get a learner's permit. I spend weeks studying the manual. As the day approaches for me to take the test I become filled with anxiety. I know the material, but am fearful that I will forget it. The day of the test has arrived. As I sit reading the questions at the test site, the palms of my hands become very moist. My stomach muscles feel tight. My mouth becomes dry. I read each question, but am afraid to choose an answer. Other people are in the room taking the test. They seem to be not only reading the questions, but also answering them. I try to stay focused. I tell myself, "You can do this." I take a few deep breaths. This seems to help. I go from one question to the next. Ah, I'm done. As I hand in my booklet, I say to myself, " I hope I passed."

A few weeks pass. The day has come that my test results arrive in the mail. I hold the envelope in my hand. I am hesitant to open it. What if I didn't pass? I take a deep breath and open the envelope. As I pull the piece of paper out of the envelope that will tell me if I did or didn't pass I notice that my hand begins to shake. I am so nervous. I unfold the piece of paper and begin to read it. It tells me that I did pass. I stand in awe. My hand is no longer shaking. I feel calmness throughout my body. I smile. I must go share the news with Judy.

Sharing the news that I have my learner's permit with Judy is exciting and rewarding. She encouraged me throughout the process of studying for the test. There were those moments that I thought I would never be able to do it. She was consistent with her words of encouragement, letting me know that I could do it. As I walk into her office, she looks up. I don't give her a chance to say a word. With excitement in my voice I say, "I did it. I passed the test. I now have a learner's permit." A smile appears on her face. Her warm, soft, gentle eyes tell me that she is just as excited as I.

Throughout the next several months Judy would give me driving lessons. The very first time being on the highway was scary. The cars move so quickly. There are so many rules to remember about driving. I'm afraid that I will get into an accident. Judy assures me that I am doing fine. She never raises her voice. She speaks calmly. As time passes and lessons are given, I begin to feel more confident about driving. I make an appointment to take my driving test. The day has arrived to take the test. As I sit in the vehicle waiting for instructions from the person who will be testing my driving capabilities, I feel confident. I feel self-assured. I know that I can do this.

A few weeks pass. The envelope arrives that will tell me if I passed my driving test. I am excited. Without hesitation I tear open the envelope. I reach inside to pull out the piece of paper. I become anxious. What if I didn't pass? Before reading it, I close my eyes and take a deep breath. I slowly open my eyes and focus on the piece of paper. It tells me that I am now a licensed driver in New York State. I am ecstatic. I feel a tear run down my cheek. It is not a tear of sadness, but a tear of accomplishment. I did it!

My birthday and holidays were very difficult for me. Most times, others who were also residing at the Y.W.C.A. would go home to spend time with family and friends. Although I was happy for each of them to be able to return to their families to celebrate and enjoy the festive seasons, I would feel abandoned. Often times I would sit in my room and cry. I would ask, "Why can't I have a family?" Although I made a choice to sever those family ties, I still wanted to be able to feel that I had a family. I wanted to feel like I belonged. Although I would try to hide the pain that I felt, Judy often times would sense that "something was up for me." In her own gentle, comforting way, she would encourage me to use my voice. Over time, I would be able to put those thoughts and feelings into words.

Throughout time my relationship with Sam and Judy would become stronger and deeper. Often, Sam and Judy would invite me to celebrate Thanksgiving with them. Although both Sam and Judy's extended family were present, I never felt "out of place." I always felt welcomed. I would no longer find myself sitting in my room asking the question, " Why can't I have a family?" Instead, I would count my many blessings. I felt as though my relationship with Sam and Judy had developed into a kinship. I felt closer to them than I had to any of my family members. I trusted them. I cared about them. I knew that they cared about me.

I spent a good many years struggling with the word "family" and all its connotations. I learned at a very young age that I needed my family. I was told at a very young age that anything that happened within the "family" was not to be shared with others. If I were to share, Dad would go to jail or I would be taken away. I was taught that secrecy was important. I was taught that secrecy was mandatory. Somewhere along the way I was given the message that if you didn't have a family, you didn't have anything. Now, I begin to think about the notion of choosing my own family. The thought is intriguing. After all, the word "family" is just a label. I was "born into a family." I was given a family name. I had no choice in the matter. I would also come to realize that my "family history" was just that. It was the history of my family of which I was a part of. It did not dictate who I was. It did not dictate what I could or couldn't do. It did not dictate who I would become. At this point in my life, I knew that the sky was the limit. I knew that there wasn't anything that I wasn't capable of doing.

At the time of the writing of this book, I have known Sam and Judy for thirty-two years. Although each of us has chosen different paths, we periodically connect with one another. I still feel warm and fuzzy inside when I am with them. It's like reuniting with a close friend or family member that you haven't seen in years. It was in developing my relationship with both Sam and Judy that I began to choose my own family. No longer do I feel inferior because I don't have a biological family. As in times that have passed, there is still no lull in conversation when we come together. The words flow easily. I am so very grateful for the difference that you both made in my life.

Sam, you were instrumental in restoring my faith and trust in men. I learned early on in our relationship that it was possible to feel safe with a man. I learned through our relationship that "good guys" do exist. Thank you! I so much appreciate, when I reflect upon past conversations that we have had, your willingness to allow me to voice my own opinion or belief. Although, often times, we would disagree with one another, you were always open to listen to what I had to say. This had a great impact on me. Over time I would come to realize that my opinion was important. Lastly, thank you for being a part of my life.

Judy, your presence in my life has had such a profound effect. As I write, I ask myself, "How does one pay tribute to someone who has taken me from crayons to perfume?" By example, you exposed me to the many gifts and lessons that life had to offer. You demonstrated many unwavering acts of kindness. Your ability to be straightforward in many ways encouraged me to look deep within myself. In doing so, I would find many answers to unanswered questions. Your patience and sensitivity in allowing "life" to unfold for me was appreciated. Although there were those times that I would make unwise decisions, I never once felt that you were being judgmental. You consistently helped me to recognize that there wasn't a goal that was beyond my reach. The gift of your example of unconditional love is priceless. Over the years, as life has unfolded, I have held

41

onto those lessons and gifts that you have given to me. In giving freely and by being an example, you made a difference in my life. My dear friend, thank you!

Chapter Seven

Making A Difference

The winter of 1973 would be spent reflecting and setting goals for myself. During this time period it becomes clear to me that I want to make a difference in the lives of others even though I don't have a clue how I am going to do this, I make a commitment to the world and myself to make a difference in some way.

In January it seemed that my circle of acquaintances and support people were talking about goals. Some were talking about new goals. Some were talking about redefining previous goals. This was a new concept for me. What had been true for me throughout the years was that surviving from one day to the next had been my only goal in life. To be able to conceptualize that life went beyond everyday survival was such a gift. I begin to ask myself, "What are my goals?" I begin to think about the possibility of volunteering at the detention center where I was detained. I reflect upon my life in general. I hadn't realized until recently that formulating a goal was possible. It becomes clear to me that I lived a very sheltered life in many ways for nineteen years. I wasn't given permission or the opportunity to formulate my own goals. Heck, before now, I didn't know goals existed. It is in reflecting and defining my goals that I also discover that life itself for me has become a privilege. I get to make choices. I get to decide what goals I want.

Mid-winter I begin to seriously think about the possibility of volunteering at the detention center. I share my thoughts and desire about this with other people. I'm told time after time by a number of people that I could make a difference in the day and life of our youth. I'm encouraged to call the detention center. Although I don't completely understand why it is that people think I can make a difference, what I do know is that I can relate to youth who are being detained on many levels. I make the call to the detention center. I speak with the person who is in charge. I share with this person the purpose and goal of my call. I talk about some of the possible activities that I might be able to offer. I am told that I can volunteer. We set up a weekly schedule. I hang up the receiver. I am elated.

Prior to making the call to the detention center, I am anxious. For weeks I contemplate making the call. Although I have a burning desire to do this, I have my doubts that I will be allowed to volunteer. After all, I am a former juvenile delinquent. I spent many months being detained at the home. I was in and out of family court. I ask myself, "Why would they let me volunteer?" I then ask myself, "Why wouldn't they let me volunteer?" I know that this is what I want to do. I know that I could possibly give hope and encouragement to youth who are being detained. I know that I could be a good role model. I know that I want to make a difference. The positives outweigh the negatives. Rather than allowing myself to dwell on the " negatives" I focus on my goal. In doing so, I begin my life long journey of making a difference.

Throughout the next several months I use my spare time to seek out other ways in which I can be of service to others within my community. I discover a volunteer program that is being offered through the local Probation Department. The aim of the program is to show kids who are in trouble that someone cares. Those who volunteer try to provide the youth with an "alternative to authoritarian relationships with adults." When I learned of the program I was impressed. It felt as though the program was tailored for me. I agreed with the goal. After all, I had experienced being in a detention center. I experienced first hand what it was like to become part of the Family Court system. I experienced what it was like to have no self-confidence. I knew from my own past experience what it was like not to trust anyone who had authority. I had begun to realize that my past experiences were in many ways a gift. I no longer looked at those experiences as negatives, but looked at them as a way of paving a path for me. Instead of becoming cynical, I looked at my experiences as a way to grow. I began to realize that my past experiences were just that, "past experiences." I would not let them dictate to me who I was or who I was to become. In deciding to become a volunteer for the program I was determined to give Cindy, the youth with whom I worked with, the message loud and clear, "I care."

During the fall a reporter approached me from The Daily Orange, the student published paper at Syracuse University, and asked if I would be willing to be interviewed. The goal was to get the word out about the Volunteers in Probation. It was also a way to recruit volunteers. Initially, I was reluctant. I thought, "What could I possibly say to recruit volunteers." After thinking about it for a couple of days, I decide to let him interview me. In agreeing to be interviewed it gave me the opportunity to share with the general public how important it is for youth to feel and know that they are being heard.

Probation workers pass word to kids in trouble

By STUART MARQUES

"The most important thing is knowing that somebody cares," said Cathy, a 19-year-old former "juvenile delinquent." "You start to think 'Well if nobody cares, what am I living for?'"

Showing kids in trouble that somebody cares is the aim of the Volunteers in Probation program, of which Cathy is a member.

The nation-wide program, begun in the Midwest 10 years ago, started last June in Syracuse. According to Kevin Harrigan, a co-ordinator of the program, the 26 volunteers work on a one-to-one basis with 15-year-olds who are on probation.

The volunteers try to provide the kids with an "alternative to an authoritarian relationship with adults," something Harrigan claims these kids have never known.

The volunteer program was begun by a group of inner-city ministers and is run by community residents in coordination with the Onondaga County Juvenile Probation Department. Besides Cathy, volunteers in the program include local business people, a retired school teacher and several SU students, Harrigan said.

Before joining the volunteer probation program two months ago, Cathy did volunteer work at Hillbrook Detention Home, where she had been an inmate several years ago.

"I quit when they gave me a set of keys. I just couldn't take locking kids in a small, tiny room, she said. "I couldn't stand seeing the kids peering through the heavily screened windows at me when I went home every day. I could have stood there and cried," the slender girl said.

"Jail doesn't do anybody any good," she continued. Cathy has an 18-year-old brother currently doing four years in prison and a friend who has just finished a two-year term. "It hasn't done them any good. It has only made them worse."

Cathy meets with "her kid," Cindy, for at least two hours a week, the minimum time required by the Volunteer program. Besides just talking with Cindy, Cathy takes her to play in volleyball games at the YWCA, and tries to get her involved with other people.

"She doesn't have any friends," Cathy said about Cindy, "and she is always being put down by other kids at school." By getting Cindy involved with other people her age, Cathy hopes to build the girl's self-confidence.

Cathy's personal brushes with the law began when she ran away from home at age 16. She spent three months in Hillbrook and was placed in a boarding home. "I just couldn't get along with my parents at all," she said.

After a short while, she ran away from the boarding home and hitch-hiked to California. On the return trip, Cindy was arrested in Indiana and sent home.

She was sent to Hillbrook again as soon as she got back in Syracuse and the court let her live with friends. After four months, during which time her friends "got mixed up with drugs," she decided to move again.

She became friends with Sister Constance Egan who worked for the juvenile court and several other people who demonstrated their concern. "When I realized that

somebody really cared about me, that's when I started to get myself together," she said.

"I knew I wanted to be involved with other people and decided to get out of there and get myself an education."

Rather than be ashamed of the troubles she has gone through, Cathy thinks they have been a learning experience. "Everything I have been through has taught me a lot," she said.

She knows that just talking isn't enough. "It's easy for kids to "turn off" advice from other," she said. "I never listened to Sister Constance, but things she kept saying over and over finally sunk in. I finally began to listen. Cindy is the same way at times. Just like a brick wall."

But she persists. "I wanted people to show me they cared about me, and I do volunteer work because I want to show Cindy I care."

It was in extending myself and doing volunteer work in my community that I was able to reap many gifts. Each time I extended and gave of myself, I was rewarded. I could see the appreciation in the eyes of those with whom I worked. I witnessed first hand the growth of those individuals' self-esteem. It was in giving that I, too, was able to grow. It was in giving that I was able to make a difference.

Chapter Eight

Challenging Myself

In the fall of 1973 I would become a part-time student at Onondaga Community College. Although I was insecure and unsure of my ability to learn, I challenged myself. In doing so, I would once again discover that nothing was beyond my reach. I would also discover that I had much more in common with my classmates than not.

I spent the winter months working with a volunteer in preparation to take the High School Equivalency Diploma examination that would be offered later in the year. It would be mid-spring that I would learn that I could attend the local college without having my high school diploma. Upon completion of twenty-six credit hours, I then would be issued my High School Equivalency Diploma. The thought of going to college excited me. It seemed to make more sense to attend the college and earn credits not only for my diploma, but also towards a degree. I no longer wanted to be tutored. I wanted to go to college.

Upon completion of all the necessary paperwork I was accepted into the Human Services curriculum. Although I was excited, I was also scared. I had no idea how I as a student was supposed to act. I wondered if the other students would like me. I wondered if I would like them. I wondered if there would be other students who worked during the day and attended classes at night. My friends and acquaintances that were already attending college let me know throughout the summer months that I would "fit right in." Although I was receiving a lot of encouragement from folks, I was still quite insecure by the time September rolled around and classes began.

The first semester would be quite the challenge for me. I hadn't given much thought prior to starting school that taking classes would require a lot of time and energy on my part. Actually, I thought all I would need to do is go to class, listen to the professor, take a test every so often and then leave. It wasn't like that at all. My classmates and I were required to do much reading; articles, chapters upon chapters in the textbooks and yes, there were those required research papers. I hadn't a clue how to even begin to research the material for a research paper, let alone write a paper. The overwhelming feeling of all that was required almost put me over the edge. For a moment I came close to throwing in the towel. As I sat on the wooden bench between the academic building and library on a cool autumn day I contemplated giving up all that my heart desired. I almost gave in to my insecurities. As I sat and thought about how I felt I could feel the warmth of my tears rolling down my cheeks. I thought to myself, "I want to do this. I can't give up." As I sat and reflected I also came to realize that my classmates were struggling as much as I. Often times, I would hear someone say, " I can't do this work." Knowing this helped me put things into perspective. As I sat on the bench and continued to reflect, my insecurities began to melt away. I once again felt as though I could do this. I once again felt as though I wanted to do this. I began to feel as though I had something in common with my classmates. I was struggling with all the demands of being a student, but so were they.

The first semester was indeed a challenge for me. I didn't drop any of my classes and although my grades weren't those of an honor role student, I passed both classes. I was proud. I was ready for the next semester.

Although I still felt insecure and challenged academically, the proceeding semesters seemed to get easier. Out of desperation and determination I developed good study skill habits. I would also become friends with some of my classmates. This was such a gift for me. As time passed and relationships developed I would discover that each of us had similar goals; that each of us had things in common; that each of us was struggling to complete the course work not only because we wanted a degree, but also because we wanted to make a difference. I felt connected to them. I felt self-assured. We would do fun things together, but we would also study and prepare for upcoming exams. When research papers were due, we would help one another out. We would brainstorm and come up with interesting topics to write about and then make suggestions to one another as to where we might find reading material to support our paper. Having to research and write a paper would always be a challenge, but over time my confidence grew and it would become less of a challenge for me. There were those moments throughout many semesters that I would feel those muscles in my stomach tighten because I knew I had to do yet another research paper. I would sit, take a few deep breathes and reflect upon all that I had done. It would take but only a moment for me to realize that yes, I can do this.

I along with my classmate and friend Marg would wait until the night before a paper was due to type it. This would mean no sleep for either one of us. Although all the material was gathered, it still needed to be typed. For me that meant pecking away for hours. A typist I was not. Marg and I would call one another every hour on the hour throughout the night, making sure that neither one of us decided to sleep rather than completing the paper. Morning would come and both our papers would be complete. I would feel so relieved. Rather than waiting for mid-day both Marg and I would drop off our completed research papers first thing in the morning and then go to breakfast. Although we were both exhausted it seemed as though we both got a spurt of energy. At breakfast we would sit and talk for hours about how relieved we were to have the paper done. It didn't seem as though we had been up for more than twenty-four hours.

As I sit and reflect upon those early years of college life, I am so very grateful to my friends and classmates. I not only was able to encourage you, but you, too, were able to encourage me. Your support and encouragement throughout those tough semesters was very much appreciated. We were individuals with our own goals, but we were able to come together to support one another. I learned many lessons, not all of which were academic in nature. I was able to reap the benefits of challenging myself. I was also able to reap the benefits of being a student.

Eventually, I graduated from Onondaga Community College and received my Associate degree in Applied Science. I felt proud. I felt a sense of accomplishment on the day of commencement. It would be a number of years later that I would work towards completion of my undergraduate work. Throughout this time period there would be those moments that I thought, "I just can't do this." In those moments I would reflect upon how difficult it was for me academically in the past. Instead of dwelling on the difficulty I chose to focus on my accomplishment. This seemed to be enough to push me along. Yes, I would receive my Bachelor of Arts degree. Commencement day for me was a day of joy. It was a day of self-fulfillment. It was a day that I smiled from ear to ear. I was proud. As I walked to the platform to receive my degree I thought to myself, " I did it. Yahoo!"

Chapter Nine

The Last Encounter

The unanswered question would fester deep within me. At the age of nineteen I wanted to know why my stepfather sexually abused me? He and I would come face to face. The answer that I would receive was not what I had hoped it would be.

Life was going well for me. I had a job. I had friends. I was happy. Although all these things were a part of my life, I didn't feel whole. I didn't feel complete. Time after time the question would surface, "Why did he sexually abuse me?" For a number of years I ignored the question and all the feelings that it encompassed. The question began to surface more often. It was becoming more of a challenge to contain all those feelings that I held deep within my soul. I wanted to know why? I wanted to know if he felt bad? I wanted an apology. It became my quest to get those unanswered questions answered.

On a warm summer day in July of 1974 as I drive to Dad's place of employment, I am very aware of the tension I feel throughout my body. When I am forced to stop at each intersection, I notice that my knees are shaking. I notice that the palms of my hands are sweating profusely. I can feel my heart pulsate. A few short city blocks away from my destination, I pull over. I feel as though I am loosing control. I know I must calm down. I take some deep breaths. I feel scared. I want to scream. Instead, I sit and cry. It feels as though the tears will never stop flowing. My head becomes filled with many thoughts. I know that he can't hurt me. I know that I want and need some answers. I know that I have to do this. After what seems to be a very long time, I am able to regain my composure. My knees aren't shaking. The palms of my hands are moist. The beat of my heart has returned to its natural rhythm. I take a long deep breath and continue the short drive.

As I sit in the driver's seat in the parking lot waiting for him, I become anxious. Many thoughts begin to fill my head. What if he tries to do something sexual to me? No, I won't let him touch me. What if he tells me that he loves me? I won't listen to those words. As a child those words were important to me. Now, as an adult they are "simply" words with no emotional attachments. What if he won't give me an answer? I'll tell him to get out of the car and drive away. I take a deep breath and tell myself, "I can do this. He can't hurt me."

I'm sitting in the car. I see Dad exit the building. He scans the parking lot. He spots me and walks toward the car. Rather than coming to the driver's side, he walks to the passenger side of the car. He grasps the handle of the door. As the door opens, I can feel my body become tense. I hear the echo of the door closing. I hadn't noticed before this that Dad was in the car. I look at him. He looks as though he has aged, since I last saw him. He has dark circles under his eyes. The wrinkles on his forehead and face are much more pronounced than I remember. He looks at me and says, " Hi." In return, I say, "Hi." He reaches for me. I don't reciprocate. Instead, I pull away and say, "Don't touch me." He looks surprised by my reaction. He says, "I've missed you."

I'm not sure how to react. I don't want to upset him. I want the answers that I came for. A few seconds pass. Although I have rehearsed this very moment in my head at least a hundred times before today, thoughts and feelings surface. In that time period I realize that I too have missed him. There is a part of me that would like to fall into his arms and submit myself to him. In a moment's

time I am able to refocus. What he did all those years to me was wrong. I want to know why. I turn to him and ask, "Why did you sexually abuse me?" He has this surprised look on his face. He lowers his head. I don't think he expected me to ask such a question. I ask again, "Why did you sexually abuse me?" He lifts his head, looks at me and says, "I loved you." I say, "Why?" He looks at me and says, " You looked like your mother." I break the eye contact and look straight ahead. A few seconds pass. No words are spoken. I am so angry. How dare him take advantage of me? How dare him sexually abuse me for all those years? How dare him say it was because I looked like my mother? I want him out of the car. I want to leave. I turn and look at him. He looks sad. He looks tired. He looks old. I make eye contact with him and say, "I need to leave." He has tears in his eyes. He looks at me and says, "Cathy, I love you." I think to myself, no you don't love me; you loved what I could do for you. I look at him and say, "Goodbye." He reaches for the handle to open the car door. I just want to push him out of the car. As he exits the car he attempts to make eye contact with me. I turn my head in the opposite direction. I am so angry. I feel like vomiting. As he walks from the car to re-enter his place of employment, I watch his every move. His head is not held high, but lowered. He walks slowly. He doesn't look back. As he enters the building I say to myself, "How dare you! How could you do this to me? How could you do this to my Mom?"

I pull out of the parking lot. I feel somewhat disoriented. A few short city blocks away I feel as though I am loosing control of my body movements. I pull the car over. My knees are shaking. I feel sick to my stomach. My heart is pulsating. My body begins to tremble. I, begin to sob uncontrollably. My head is filled with so many feelings, thoughts and memories. I wanted him to tell me that he was sorry. I wanted him to tell me that it wasn't my fault. I didn't want to hear that he sexually abused me because I looked like my mother. How could I as a child look like an adult? His answer makes no sense to me. How dare him tell me that he loves me! How dare him not take responsibility for his actions! The only person he loves is himself. The only person he cares about is himself.

It seems as though I've been sitting in the car for hours. I glance at my watch; a half-hour has passed. I am no longer sobbing. My knees aren't shaking. My body isn't trembling. My stomach has calmed down. I don't feel like vomiting. My heartbeat has returned to its natural rhythm. I feel as though I have control of my mind and body. Although I am disappointed with the information that I was given, I am grateful for the encounter. Before starting the engine I fold my hands, take a long deep breath and thank God for giving me the strength and opportunity to come face to face with my stepfather this one last time.

It would be a number of years after much time, energy and money was spent on my own therapy that I was able to fully appreciate that last encounter I had with my stepfather. Prior to engaging in therapy, I thought I was being very selfish in asking him, "Why, did you sexually abuse me?" A part of me didn't feel that it was my place to ask questions and yet another part of me felt that after all was said and done, the reality was, he took care of me all those years. Over time I was able to work through my confusion and pain. I came to realize that it took a lot of determination and courage on my part to confront him. It was then that I would also come to realize that although my stepfather's response was not what I wanted to hear, the encounter would leave me with a sense of resolution and acceptance.

Chapter Ten

Isabell

 As life continued to unravel for me there would be many gifts and lessons. I would be introduced to Isabell Daley Conklin, a woman whom I would never forget. Over time our relationship would develop into a deep rich love and respect for one another. We would become housemates. We would become friends. She would become my mentor. She would become the grandmother that I always wanted. She would become my surrogate mother. Together we would journey down life's path. She was one of those unexplainable mysterious gifts that life had to offer. I would come to realize over time that it wasn't a coincidence that we were both to meet. It was a gift. Her presence in my life would have a life long profound effect.

We would meet in September of 1976. An acquaintance of mine had told me about this wonderful older woman who lost her husband to cancer and was looking for a student to live in her home. I was going to school part-time and working. I was on a fixed income. Money was tight. I was told that money wasn't the reason that she wanted someone to live in her home. What she wanted and needed was companionship. She was still grieving for her husband. She was lonely in the big house by herself. Although she had two daughters who were married and had families of their own, they were not local residents, but lived in other states. It felt as though she and I already had a few things in common. I certainly knew what it was like to grieve the loss of someone you loved. I too wanted and needed companionship. I decided that I would call her to set up a day and time for us to meet one another.

Before my finger touched the doorbell the door opened. This woman who had a warm gentle smile greeted me. Her face radiated warmth and it seemed as though her eyes had a twinkle to them. I let her know that I was looking for Mrs. Conklin. She responded by telling me that she was Mrs. Conklin. I had expected to meet a woman who was frail and depressed. I hadn't expected to meet a woman whose aura was that of warmth. I hadn't expected to meet a woman who seemed to be happy. As we sat conversing with one another in the front room of her home, the words just seemed to flow. It didn't feel as though either one of us spent any time thinking about what we should or shouldn't say. Our conversation felt natural. It felt good. We both decided that we were a "fit." I would move in on the weekend. I left feeling ecstatic. I liked her energy. I liked her outlook on life. I liked her.

As fall turned to winter and winter into spring our relationship too would evolve, as did the seasons. Within six months we were calling one another friend. It felt good. It felt natural. By mid-spring I decided that I wanted Isabell to meet some of my other friends. Actually, some of my friends were curious about this person who I talked so much about. They wanted to meet her. She, too, wanted to meet them. I thought it would be a good idea to have a dinner party. When I talked to Isabell about this she was excited and wanted very much to meet some of my friends. In all the time spent in preparation for this get together I never gave any thought to not serving wine at dinner. The food was going to be good and I thought it would also be nice to serve a good bottle of wine. An hour before guest arrived Isabell approached me and said, "I don't allow spirits in my home." I had absolutely no idea what she was talking about. Rather than asking her what she meant I said, "Okay." I proceeded to set the table, placing a wine glass at each setting. Isabell once again approached me and said, "I don't allow spirits in my home." I thought to myself, "What the heck is she talking about? As far as I knew none of my friends worship the devil." I then realized that I didn't understand what she was talking about. Rather than ignoring what she said, I asked her what she meant. She told me, "I don't allow alcohol in my home." I chuckled to myself, turned to her, smiled and said, "I thought you were trying to tell me that you didn't allow devil worshippers in your home. I had no idea that you were referring to alcohol." She smiled and said, "Being a Baptist minister's wife I've never allowed alcohol in my home." I let her know that this was not a problem. Rather than removing the wine goblets from the table we decided that we would use them for the water. The evening was filled with laughter. Stories were shared. There was no need for alcohol to be served. At the end of the evening Isabell and my other friends could now place a face with a name. A quarter of a century has passed since this memorable evening. I was experienced in some areas of life and yet so naïve in other areas. Every so often when I hear the word 'spirits' I chuckle and think of her.

When spring arrived there was always a sense of renewal that radiated from Isabell. She would become so excited at the first sight of a crocus popping up in the yard. She made it a point to share this with me and called all her friends to let them know. Her excitement reminded me of the excitement you see in the eyes of a child who has just discovered what gifts are. For Isabell, the gift wasn't a materialistic one, but a gift of nature and the promise of spring to follow. As our relationship developed, I became just as excited as she to see the first crocus appear. We were like two kids awaiting the first sign of spring after the long winter months.

We had an area in the backyard that we used for a vegetable garden. In mid-May of each year I would turn over the soil in preparation for planting. Isabell and I had an agreement. I would prepare the soil and she would plant and take care of the garden throughout the season. The first couple of years it was quite a challenge for me to complete this task. As I was growing up as a kid and on into young adulthood I hadn't become familiar with any of the vegetable garden lingo. I had no idea what "good planting soil" was. Isabell told me that the soil in the backyard was rich in minerals. I never thought to ask her why that was. Initially, all I focused on was completing my task of turning over the soil. Although the area is large, the soil is moist and easy to turn over with a shovel. My attire consisted of sneakers, shorts and a tee shirt. What I would discover after only a short time of digging and turning over the soil was that the critters that lived just beneath the top layer of soil were much bigger than I thought. Although they were much smaller than I, the thought of one of them crawling on me was scary. I tried to ignore the huge worms, but each time I saw one of them slithering across the fresh turned soil I would jump and let out a little scream. Isabell at one point heard me and came rushing down the stairs leading to the backyard. She asked, "Cathy are you okay?" I was embarrassed. I hadn't thought that anyone had heard me. I looked at her with tears in my eyes and said, "I don't like these huge worms. They scare me." With concern and compassion in her voice she said, "Cathy, it is because of these huge earth worms that we have rich soil." She went on to say, that they couldn't and wouldn't hurt me. In an instant I remembered the words that she spoke earlier in the day, "The soil in the backyard is rich in minerals." I now knew what she meant. In the years to follow, as I would turn over the soil in preparation for planting, I still didn't want any of the critters to crawl on me. Over time I developed an appreciation for those critters that live just beneath the soil. Instead of jumping back and letting out a scream, I stand and watch, as they travel across the freshly turned soil. I have come to realize that they, too, have a purpose.

Although Isabell was very grounded in her faith, she wasn't the type of person who would preach at you. I was very thankful for this. The lessons that were learned from this very wise and gifted person were acts of every day kindness. It seemed as though she lived her life to make a difference in the lives of others. I was educated in the Catholic faith. She was educated in the American Baptist Church. She had been married to a Baptist minister until his death in 1975, and supported his ministry. She was committed to her faith. I on the other hand felt that I was dictated to as I was growing up. Although my faith sustained me, I desired something deeper and much more meaningful. I no longer wanted or needed someone to tell me what to think or how to feel in regards to my faith. I was in my early twenties. I was searching for a more meaningful relationship with my maker. I was searching for inner peace. She and I on occasion would have lengthy conversations about our beliefs. We would share our thoughts and feelings, neither of us being judgmental about what the other thought or felt. As time passed she became much more then a friend to me. She became my mentor. I looked up to her. I respected and admired her for her sensitivity towards others, for her deep rooted faith in God, for her never ending ability to look for the good in others. I would come to realize through stories that she would share and her every day examples that one didn't need to allow anger to fester deep within one's self. Being angry and staying angry was a choice, not fate. I would come to realize that in forgiving others, I could then forgive myself. I would come to realize that tears weren't a sign of weakness, but a sign of strength.

Although I was hesitant to share much about my past in regards to my family it seemed as though Isabell knew and at times could feel the pain that I held deep within me. I had a longing. I wanted to feel as though I belonged. I wanted a family. I had shared with Isabell that when I was a baby my mother died of polio. She recalled the memories that she had of the time that the outbreak of polio had taken place. She shared some of the fears and concerns that she and others had. As she spoke of her memories and fears her eyes filled with tears. She voiced that it was a very scary time in her life. She talked about boiling water and taking many precautions to protect herself and her family. As I listened as she shared her memories, tears rolled down my cheeks. I glanced at her and turned away quickly, trying to hide my tears. I noticed that she too, had tears rolling down her cheeks. Over the years we would have many conversations that involved sharing our feelings and memories. We would talk about our past disappointments. We would talk about our regrets. We would talk about our hopes and dreams. As time passed and our relationship evolved, we became closer.

One day, as we were talking, Isabell let me know that it felt as though I was one of her daughters. When I heard these words spoken I didn't know what to say. It wasn't that I didn't like what I was hearing, but I couldn't believe what I was hearing. Who would want me for their daughter? I didn't have many fun filled memories of growing-up to share. I was struggling to deal with my past issues and maintain a positive attitude. I came from a dysfunctional family. Many thoughts and feeling rushed through my body for those few minutes. I looked at Isabell and was able to find the words to express the feelings that I felt within myself. I let her know that she couldn't be my mother because my mother was dead. I went on to say that if I allowed her to be my mother, a part of me would feel as though I turned my back on my mom. I let her know that I couldn't do this. Isabell sits and listens. As tears roll down my cheeks, I share with her that she is the best thing that ever happened to me. I begin to cry. I let her know that I love her very much. Isabell has tears rolling down her face. We reach for one another. We make contact. I hold on to her. She holds on to me. After a few minutes we are both able to regain control of ourselves. I look at her and let her know that I never knew my grandmother and that I would feel comfortable and very pleased if she would be my grandmother. As I turned my head to look into her eyes, I could see the happy expression on her face and the twinkle in her eyes. She said without hesitation, "Grandma, I am." Those words were like music to my ears. From that day forward I no longer felt that I didn't belong. From that day forward I felt that I did have a family.

Although I wasn't able to allow myself to give permission to Isabell to take on the role of becoming my mother, in reality she did become my surrogate mom. At the time, I felt had I given her this label, I would have been disloyal to my biological mother. Although she and I never discussed it again, I would attend the annual mother

60

and daughter celebration at her church on a yearly basis. It was an event that we both looked forward to. She would introduce me to her friends and parishioners as her daughter. Hearing those words made me feel warm and fuzzy inside. I was happy. I was proud.

As a young child my great escape was to watch the weekly television show Lassie. Lassie became my hero. The love, loyalty, courage, and compassion he and Timmy shared helped me to forget for a short period of time all that was going on around me. As I sat and watched the half-hour show I would pretend that I was with Lassie instead of Timmy being with him. I longed for a relationship similar to the one that Timmy had with his parents. The half-hour show filled an empty, hollow space within me. Although the longing for a relationship that Timmy had with his parents would remain a dream, I held onto the hope that one day I, too, would own a dog like Lassie. Many years later I would fulfill that hope. I, too, would own Lassie.

On the morning of January 5, 1981 I would hold a newborn pup in the palm of my hand. It was a collie. He was so tiny. He was so cute. I immediately reflected upon my great memories of watching Lassie on television as a child. I knew in an instant that he was going to be my dog. What I hadn't yet figured out was how I was going to approach Isabell to ask if I could bring a puppy home. Although she and I had talked about many things, we never talked about having an animal in the house. The subject never came up.

Upon my return to my office I immediately call Isabell. As I sit at my desk dialing the number, I wonder what she will say. I hear her voice. She says, " Hello." I respond by saying, "Isabell, this is Cathy." She says, "Hi." I'm silent for a moment. I'm not at all sure what to say. She breaks the silence and says, "Cathy, are you okay?" I'm able to refocus. I say, "Isabell, I need to talk with you. I am coming home for lunch." She says, "I will prepare lunch. What time will you arrive?" I let her know that this is not necessary. She insists that she will make lunch. She goes on to say, "You work long days and you must keep your strength up." I knew by the tone in her voice that there was no way that I would be able to talk her out of making lunch for me. I let her know that I will be home at noon. As I hang up the receiver I wonder, will she say, yes?

As I drive the short distance home for lunch, I pray the entire way. I envision this little puppy in my arms. I wonder what I will name him? As I pull into the driveway, reality bestows its presence on me. Before exiting the car, I ask God, "Please let her say, yes."

As I enter the house and begin to walk toward the kitchen I notice that Isabell is sitting in the green chair in the living room. I toss my coat over one of the chairs and walk toward her. I can feel my stomach muscles begin to tighten. I look at her. She looks at me with that warm smile that I am so accustomed to. This is good; I would rather ask her before we eat lunch. Instead of just coming out and popping the question, I let her know that I was at a foster home this morning and held a newborn collie puppy in the palm of my hand. I let her know that he was so cute. I went on to say that I always wanted a collie. I wasn't able to contain the excitement that was bubbling over within me. Before I knew it the rest of the words just flowed. I asked her if I could bring the puppy home when he was old enough? To my surprise without hesitation she said, "Cathy, anything for you." I was ecstatic. My long held dream of owning my own collie was coming true.

Throughout the next ten weeks it wasn't difficult to stay excited about the pup. I would venture out to see him at least once a week. It was fun watching him play with his siblings. It was fun sitting on the floor and letting him jump on me. It seemed as though he knew that eventually he would be leaving his mother and siblings. It was though we both gravitated toward one another on each of my visits. Each visit it became increasingly harder for me to leave. I knew this was because I had bonded with him. I purchased a few books on how to care for a collie. Although my dream was to one day own a collie, I had absolutely no idea how to care for one. After doing my research I would realize that the care of an animal required much more than just feeding and walking. It would require a commitment. This was a new concept for me. Up to now, the closest thing to a commitment for me was to share my life with Isabell. I wasn't one to look too far ahead. Owning and caring for a dog would change that part of my

life. I no longer could just concern myself with making decision for just myself, but I would also need to think about and plan for this new addition that would soon be very much a part of my life. Isabell shared my excitement. We spent some time talking about and making plans for the pup. We had to figure out where he would be most comfortable during the day. The basement would be a safe place while I was at work. When it got warm enough outside, he could stay in the garage while I was at work. He would sleep in my room at night.

The day has finally arrived to bring the pup home. Excitement fills the air. Isabell has found the hot water bottle. She told me a couple of weeks ago that for the first couple of nights we should fill it with warm water, wrap a towel around it and place it in the box where the pup will sleep. He will feel the warmth from the hot water bottle and think that he is sleeping next to his mom. We were able to find an old alarm clock that would also be placed in the box. As the clock ticks throughout the night he will think that it is his mother's heartbeat. Both the hot water bottle and the alarm clock would be lifesavers. I thought for sure at least for the first couple of nights that he would cry and yelp for his mom, but he didn't. He was content and grew accustomed to my arm dangling in his box on a nightly basis.

Isabell and Asher
March 1981

As the days, weeks, months and years passed, Asher would bring much joy into my life. His unconditional love would help me to thrive. In thriving, I, too, was able to give to others unconditionally. The depth of his loyalty to me was something that I had never experienced with another human being. He helped me to rekindle the belief that reliability and dependability did still exist. There were those times in my life when I wasn't feeling very self-assured. I wanted to throw in the towel, just because it would have been the easiest and less painful way out. It was as though he could sense this. I'd look into his brown eyes and receive the message, "You must go on." The compassion that we shared for one another and life was such a special and unique gift. As he grew from a puppy on into adulthood, I, too, grew as an individual. I am so glad that I held onto that long held dream of one day owning my very own Lassie.

The kinship that Isabell and I shared was such a precious, unexplainable and unexpected gift that was given to me. She was my friend. She was my mentor. She was the grandmother that I had always hoped for. Although I resisted and was reluctant to allow her to take on the role of a surrogate mother, in reality, that was exactly what she became. Our relationship had developed into such a deep, rich love and respect for one another that it wasn't necessary to define it. What was important to both of us was that we knew what we felt in our hearts. We knew without a doubt that we had developed a kinship. On June 27, 1995, Isabell passed away. It was a day of great sadness. I would no longer be able to look into her eyes. I would no longer be able to share a smile with her. I would no longer be able to hug her and whisper in her ear, "I love you." For sometime after her death I missed these and many other memorable times we shared with one another. What I would come to realize was that all that Isabell and I had shared was not lost or gone. My heart was still filled with much love for her. I had all the fond memories that we shared. I had all those words of wisdom tucked away in my memory along with the conversations that she and I had shared. Although physically she was gone, I felt at the time of her passing as I do to this very day, that she is very much alive within me. We were then and I believe we are still connected by those heartstrings. Her spirit lives on.

Chapter Eleven

Junior

In the first book of the trilogy series entitled, Lost Innocence, I shared with the reader the closeness and some of the struggles that both Junior and I shared throughout our childhood. As adults we would grow apart from one another, making different choices and leading different lives.

Life's path would bring separate journeys for both Junior and I. We would choose different life styles. My heart would become softened by the many gifts that life had to offer. I would view life as an opportunity and precious gift. Junior would become angry and bitter, feeling that the world owed him. He would spend much of his early adult life housed in the local penitentiary. As he grew older and became educated to the life style of crime he would then be housed in various state prisons throughout the United States.

Although I did not grow accustomed to or take a liking to visiting him when he was incarcerated, locally, I did visit. After a number of arrests and incarcerations, visiting him became routine. It also became old. I would hear the same excuses over and over again. "It was the other person's fault. The police arrested the wrong person. I was set up. I didn't do anything wrong." Often times, I would feel embarrassed going to the local penitentiary to visit him. I was a law-biding citizen. With the exception of a few parking tickets that were unpaid, I had no criminal record. Although I had no criminal record I felt as though I was guilty of something by association. I began to resent the fact that each time I visited Junior he seemed to feel comfortable in his surroundings. It seemed as though he didn't mind being incarcerated. Being inside a penitentiary made me feel very uncomfortable. The guards let me in, but they also had the control and power to let me out. I wondered, "What if they don't let me out?" I felt as though I was the one making all the effort in the relationship. I was the one traveling to and from on a weekly basis to see him. His effort was minimal.

One-day reality hit me smack in the face. It became clear to me that prison life was what Junior chose. He would commit a crime; in doing so, there would be a consequence. I shared with him how I felt. He didn't agree with me at all. He felt that he did nothing wrong and was being punished for absolutely no reason. I knew that this wasn't true. In all the crimes that he committed there was enough evidence to warrant his incarceration. I let him know that I would no longer come to visit him while he was housed in a penitentiary. I shared with him that it was uncomfortable for me. I let him know that I felt as though I was a prisoner each time I visited. I no longer wanted to feel this way. Although, initially, he was not at all pleased with my decision, we both came to an agreement to write to one another on a regular basis. I left the penitentiary that day feeling proud. It had taken me well over two years to accept the way I felt and act upon my feelings and own needs in regards to the dreaded weekly visits at the local penitentiary.

As the years passed Junior would move from state to state. Often times, I wouldn't hear from him for a few years. I often wondered if he was alive? I then would receive a letter from him. The return address would be from a state prison. I welcomed the letter. I no longer needed to wonder if he was dead or alive. Unfortunately, Junior would spend most of his adult life behind prison doors, learning from other inmates the tricks of the trade of crime life. It saddened me then and saddens me now to know that he has spent most of his life behind locked doors.

We are like night and day. I have a sensitive heart. I embrace life. I look at life as a precious gift. I don't at all feel that the world owes me. I do feel as though I owe the world. Junior's heart has become hardened. He feels that the world owes him. Life for him has become one drug deal after another. Life for him has become one more heist. Life for him has become planning the next crime.

One of my strong beliefs is that change is possible for all people. It matters not the age of the person. What does matter is the person's willingness to change. I embrace this belief and hold onto the possibility that one day, Junior too, just might open himself up to all the possible gifts that life has to offer. I'm not sure that the day will arrive. The choice is his. What I choose to hold onto in the moment is the warm fuzzy feeling that I felt as a child embracing my brother on a warm sunny day. We shared laughter. We shared love. We shared a childhood. I will continue to hold onto the belief that change is possible. Perhaps, one day, he and I will once again embrace one another.

Chapter Twelve

Turmoil

During the month of January of 2000 as I sat in front of my computer attempting to finish the first book in the trilogy series, I felt much turmoil within myself. After some exploration I realized that I had some unfinished business to tend to. There was one more person that I needed to forgive. Kathy lived locally. The opportunity arose for me to come face-to-face with her. I felt confused and as though my life had absolutely no order to it leading to the day that we would come face-to-face. On that day, however, I would walk away feeling cleansed and empowered.

Although legally, Kathy would have been considered to be my stepmother, I didn't as a child and still to this day do not consider her to be my stepmother. She was a person who was a part of my life as I was growing up. As an adult I could make the choice to allow her to be a part of my life or choose not to. I chose not to. Although she wasn't a part of my life physically she remained very much a real part of my life throughout the writing of the first book in the trilogy series. Throughout the writing of Lost Innocence, I couldn't help but wonder what it might have been like for her growing up as a child. With all that I knew about abuse and neglect of children I couldn't imagine her childhood as being a healthy one. Feelings, memories and fears would surface within me. The only way I was able to continue to write was to allow myself to feel. What I would come to realize is I had the need to let Kathy know that I forgave her. With all the healing work that I had done over the years I wasn't able to forgive any of my perpetrators face to face. They had all passed away by the time I was willing and able to find forgiveness within myself for them. My forgiveness work would be done in therapy or the confines of my home. I felt that this would be a great opportunity for me. I knew it could bring great healing for me. Although I had this need to forgive her, I had no desire to develop a relationship with her. The decision to come face-to-face with her was a selfish one. I had the need to come clean with myself. I wanted to free myself of her. I knew in forgiving her, I could do just that.

The days and weeks that led up to the face-to-face meeting with Kathy would bring some turbulence. Fears, thoughts, and feelings begin to stir within me. What if she tries to hit me? What if she starts screaming at me? What if she calls the police? After taking some time to allow myself to explore these fears what I realized was the fears that were surfacing were those fears of the little girl that was once intimidated and fearful of this woman who seemed to have so much power and authority. I knew that I couldn't dwell on those old fears. I knew that I needed to change my thought process. I knew that I needed to empower myself. I begin to visualize Kathy as a woman who is kind-hearted. I begin to visualize Kathy as a woman who is humane. I begin to visualize Kathy as a woman who is tender. In doing so on a daily basis I begin to feel empowered. The fears would still surface, but as the day grew nearer to coming face-to-face with her the fears weren't as intense. I was able to acknowledge the fears and let them go. I realized that I was now an adult, no longer a child, and knew that she couldn't hurt me. I also held on to my strong belief that there wasn't anything that my God/Goddess and I couldn't do. I would spend many hours praying and seeking guidance. I knew beyond a doubt that this was the right thing to do.

As the day grew closer of that face-to-face meeting with Kathy, I came to realize that I wanted and needed support. I chose to do something, which was out of character for me. I phoned a friend and asked for support. I realized that a large part of my anxiety was that I would be venturing into Kathy's neck of the woods. I had absolutely no idea how she would respond. I hadn't seen her in twenty-nine years. The memories that I had of her were not pleasant ones. I knew that I needed to formulate a concrete plan to help myself feel safe. I knew that I needed to help that little child within me to feel as safe as possible. I didn't want to put myself in the position of having to deal with the unknown by myself. As a child I had to deal with her by myself, but as an adult I realized that I didn't need to nor did I want to deal with her on a one-to-one basis. I was very fearful that she would attempt to become verbally or physically abusive. What I asked my friend; Cherie to do was to accompany me on the morning of the face-to-face encounter with Kathy. I asked that she bring her cell phone. What I requested is that she not walk to the door with me, but to stay within ear range. If she saw that Kathy was becoming physically or verbally abusive to me, she was to call 911. A safety plan was put into place.

I awaken. It is a sunny, but cold February morning. My stomach muscles feel tight. I lay in bed, not wanting to get up. I think about what I will say to Kathy in just a few short hours from now. I begin to have second thoughts about doing this. My fears begin to kick in. I think about all the "What Ifs?" I lie in bed and pray. I ask for strength. I ask for guidance. I begin to cry. A few minutes pass. I feel calmness throughout my body. I trust that the calmness that I feel within is a sign that everything will be okay.

We pull into the parking area, not far from where Kathy lives. God, I'm so nervous. I feel my stomach muscles begin to tighten. As I exit the car I notice that my balance is off. My legs are trembling. Cherie looks at me and asks, "Are you okay?" I look at her and say, " I'm scared. My legs are shaking." We embrace one another. After what seemed to be a few minutes, but was only a few seconds, I notice that I have regained my balance. My legs are no longer trembling. My stomach muscles aren't as tight. I begin to feel calmness throughout my body. I feel the rays of the sun on my shoulders. I look at Cherie and say, "Let's go." As we walk up the sidewalk and towards Kathy's home I say to Cherie, "Do you have the cell phone on?" She assures me it is on. My foot hits the first step and then the second step. I stand in front of Kathy's door. I look to my left. I see Cherie standing about one hundred feet away. She gives me a reassuring look. I take a deep breath. I knock on the storm door. I don't get an answer. I think to myself, "She better be home." I knock again. The entrance door opens. Sure enough the person who has answered the door is Kathy. She has aged some, but looks basically the same. She doesn't recognize me, but asks in a gruff tone, "What do you want?" I reach for the handle on the storm door and open it partially. She stands in the doorway. I ask for her by her marriage name with my stepfather. She tells me, "No one lives here by that name." I am persistent. I ask for her by using her maiden name. Again, she says, "No one lives here by that name." It was obvious to me that she did not recognize me at all. As I stood on her porch looking at her I thought to myself, "No way am I going to turn around and walk away." I look at her straight in the eyes and say, " I am Cathy Brochu. I wanted to let you know that I forgive you and wish you well." The expression on her face was that of someone seeing a ghost. Her jaw dropped and for a few seconds there was silence. She broke the silence and asked, "How did you find me?" I looked at her and said, "It matters not how I found you. What does matter is that I forgive you." I was dumbfounded by her reaction, which was, "Praise be to God. I forgive you." I began to feel my blood begin to boil. How dare she say those words? She is the one that needs forgiveness. I was a child and did nothing wrong. I hear her repeat, "Praise be to God." I look at her and say, "Goodbye." I turn my body and descend down the few short steps. My feet hit the sidewalk. I am aware that I am angry. What I really want to do is run as fast as I can. I want to be as far away from her as possible. Instead, I walk. If Kathy is watching me leave I don't want her to have the impression that I am fearful of her. I want her to know that I am no longer afraid of her. Cherie is standing waiting for me. As I approach her we both reach for one another. We embrace. I feel as though I want to collapse, but I don't. We both continue to walk the short distance to the parking area. Once in the parking area and out of sight of Kathy I look at Cherie and say, "Can you believe that she had enough nerve to say, I forgive you? How dare she feel that I need forgiveness! Dam her!"

Part of what I wanted and desired was for Kathy to show some remorse. She didn't. I had hoped that she would give me an apology.

That didn't happen either. What did happen for me is that I was able to walk away feeling unburdened by unfinished business as it related to Kathy. The words that I spoke "I forgive you and wish you well" were sincere and heartfelt. I no longer felt any tension within my body. The tension that once lingered had been lifted. I walked away feeling as though I had been cleansed. I walked away feeling empowered. Knowing that I no longer needed to fear her; realizing that the power she had over me when I was a child no longer existed; knowing that the fears of the past were just that, fears of the past. Although I didn't receive an apology and it did not appear that she was remorseful I reaped many benefits. I walked away feeling proud. I walked away feeling cleansed. I walked away feeling empowered.

Chapter Thirteen

Life Is Good

    As I moved toward closure in the second of the trilogy series I reflected upon my life journey. I felt as though I had come Full Circle. In creating a Family Tree I would discover my heritage. I would break the cycle of a lineage of incest within my family. I discovered the importance of integration of self. In seeking answers I would find myself.

Family Tree

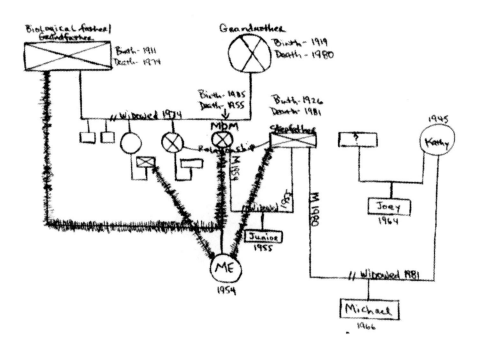

O = Female   ⚡ = Incest
▭ = Male   M = Marriage

The initial information that I was able to discover in regard to my Family Tree was not at all what I had hoped for. When I began my search I had hoped to find "someone" who might be able to share information that would help me to feel better about myself and about my heritage. I had already discovered in 1971 that my grandfather was my biological father, but held onto the possibility of discovering a relative that was healthy and normal. As my search continued I would discover that incest within my family was a common occurrence. It was perpetual, continuing from one generation to the next. I wondered, "How could this be? Why did this happen?" I was angry. I was resentful. I was embarrassed. I wanted a family.

Reality for me at the time was that I didn't have a family. Reality was that the topic of incest was not talked about openly. I knew that I wanted and needed to talk about my family heritage. I entered therapy. This for me meant that I had to prioritize, making the expense of therapy a priority. Not being able to go out to dinner, go to a movie, or go on vacation was a sacrifice, but one that I knew would reap benefits in the long run. After a number of years in therapy I was able to look at my heritage and not feel as angry, resentful, or embarrassed. I was able to accept all that I had discovered. I felt then and feel to this very day that I have made a difference within my biological family. The gift to them is that the cycle has been broken. History will not repeat its self.

As the years continued to unravel I acquired a deep appreciation of my willingness to allow myself to shed the layers of hurt that lingered within me. Prior to entering therapy I intellectualized and minimized the abuse that I experienced as a child. Often times I would say to myself, "It happened. Get over it. Move on." Although I continued to repeat those words to myself the pain and discomfort that I felt deep within did not disappear. I knew that mere determination would not fix those deep-seeded wounds. There were periods of time while I was in therapy that I just wanted to throw in the towel. The drudging up of thoughts, feelings, fears and memories felt unbearable at times. I remember thinking: "I lived and breathed my abuse. Why do I have to re-experience it by talking about it? God, how am I going to get through this?" As time passed and my healing continued the intensity of those feelings, fears, thoughts and memories dissipated. What I had come to realize was that the child within me had begun to heal. She was given permission to think, feel and react. She was acknowledged. She was honored. She was given a voice.

The exploration and integration of self would bring with it the realization that I had an option. I could pick and choose my own family. Remember in the spring of 1971 I was declared an emancipated minor. This was a decision that was set forth and made by a Family Court Judge. I was no longer bound by the legal system. I was Set Free. Although the judge had made his decision I had already made the conscious choice to never return home. I made that choice because I no longer wanted to be emotionally, physically or sexually abused. I had endured the abuse for thirteen years. In making this choice there would be a sacrifice. I would give up what I considered my family. I don't regret that healthy and wise decision, but I do miss the sense of belonging to a family.

The deep, rich and loving relationship that Isabell (Chapter Ten) and I had developed along with the exploration and integration of self helped me to realize that I had choices.

As the years continued to unravel for me I would discover that one didn't necessarily need to be " born into" a family to feel the bond that one feels when you have siblings or a family. I would meet two separate individuals on two separate occasions and over time my relationship with both of these individuals would prosper. My life would change. I went from not having a family to having not one, but two siblings. Upon mutual commitment to one another Dan would become my chosen brother and Cherie would become my chosen sister. Two separate individuals. Two separate relationships. Two separate commitments. Both these individuals have enriched my life in countless ways, as I have theirs. We have shared laughter. We have shared joy. We have shared tears. We have shared the deep pain that one feels when you've lost a loved one to death. We have shared our aspirations and been supportive to one another throughout that process. Although time constraints at times has limited our spending time with one another because each of us lead very busy lives we are trussed together by our heartstrings and commitment to one another. As I reflect upon the relationship that I have with both Dan and Cherie, I am in awe. Both entered my life at different times. Both have become a part of me as I have with them. I no longer ask the question, "Why am I so richly blessed? Instead, I count my many blessings and before drifting off to sleep I say, Thank you for my brother Dan. Thank you for my sister Cherie."

What I have found to be true is that each of us walking the earth has something in common. Each of us has "old wounds" that need to be addressed in order to live a full, happy and healthy life. It does not matter what those wounds are. What does matter is that they are wounds. For many years I experienced first hand what it was like to simply "exist." I experienced what it was like to feel shamed. I experienced what it was like to isolate myself from others because I was a victim. I experienced what it was like to live in silence. I experienced what it was like to be untrusting of others. I experienced what it was like to be stripped of my self-esteem. What is true for me is that had I not decided many years ago to take the leap of faith and consciously work diligently to integrate those childhood wounds into my life, I would not be the healthy and happy person that I am today. Dan and Cherie would not be a part of my life. I would not be making a difference in my community and other communities. I no longer live my life simply by "existing," but live a life that is full of hope for tomorrow. I am happy. I am healthy. I feel whole.

Suggested Readings

Bass, Ellen, and Laura Davis. The Courage to Heal: A Guide for Women Survivors of Child Sexual Abuse. Harper & Row, 1988.

Brady, Katherine. Father's Days: A True Story of Incest. Dell, 1979.

Brochu, Cathy. Lost Innocence: A Daughter's Account of Love, Fear and Desperation. 1stBooks, 2001.

Davis, Laura. The Courage to Heal Workbook: For Women and Men Survivors of Child Sexual Abuse. Harper & Row, 1988.

Davis, Laura. Allies In Healing: When the Person You Love Was Sexually Abused as a Child. Harper Collins Publishers, 1991.

Davis, Laura. I Thought We'd Never Speak Again: The Road from Estrangement to Reconciliation. Harper Collins Publishers, 2002.

Evert, Kathy, and Inie Bijkerk. When You're Ready: A Woman's Healing from Childhood Physical and Sexual Abuse by Her Mother. Launch Press, 1988.

Farmer, Steven. Adult Children of Abusive Parents: A Healing Program for Those Who Have Been Physically, Sexually, or Emotionally Abused. Random House, Incorporated, 1990.

Forward, Susan, and Craig Buck. Betrayal of Innocence: Incest and its Devastation. Penguin, 1988.

Graber, Ken. Ghosts in the Bedroom: A Guide for Partners of Incest Survivors. Health Communications, Incorporated, 1991.

Herman, Lewis, Judith. Father-Daughter Incest. Harvard University Press, 1981.

Lew, Mike. Victims No Longer: Men Recovering from Incest and Other Sexual Child Abuse. Harper & Row, 1990.

Miller, Alice. Thou Shalt Not Be Aware: Society's Betrayal of the Child. American Library, 1986.

Poston, Carol, and Karen Lison. Reclaiming Our Lives: Hope for Adult Survivors of Incest. Little Brown, 1989.

White, Louise. The Obsidian Mirror: An Adult Healing from Incest. Seal Press, 1988.

Resources

Child Help USA
15757 North Seventy 8th Street
Scottsdale, Arizona 85260
1-800-422-4453
Offers a 24-hour crisis hot line, national information and referral Network for support groups, therapists, and for reporting suspected abuse

The National Committee to Prevent Child Abuse (NCPCA)
P.O. Box 2866
Chicago, IL 60690
1-800-556-2722
Headquartered in Chicago, is a nonprofit organization with the goal of preventing child abuse in all forms. NCPCA promotes public education through its national media campaign, a catalog of publications, and training and technical assistance. Chapters of the national organization are located throughout the United States.

Child Welfare League of America
440 First Street, NW, Suite 310
Washington, DC 20001-2085
1-202-638-2952
Headquartered in Washington, DC. The Child Welfare League of America is a 75 year-old association of nearly 800 public and private, nonprofit agencies that serve abused, neglected and abandoned children, youth and their families. CWLA plays a major advocacy role on Capitol Hill, developing guidelines for the

provision of child welfare services, conducting research and training, and is the world's largest publisher of child welfare materials.

Survivors of Incest Anonymous
P.O. Box 190
Benson, Maryland 21018-9998
1-410-893-3322
www.siawso.org
Is a nonprofit organization with the goal to help survivors to connect with one another and carry the message of recovery to those who still suffer. It serves as a headquarters for 300 plus SIA meetings in the United States and around the world.

RAINN (Rape, Abuse & Incest National Network)
635-B Pennsylvania Ave., SE
Washington, DC 20003
1-800-656-4673
www.rainn.org
A 24-hour hotline offering confidential counseling and referrals.

The International Newsletter for Woman Survivors of Childhood Sexual Abuse
The Healing Woman Foundation
P.O. Box Z8040
San Jose, CA 95159
408-246-1788
http://www.healingwoman.org
Offers publications and support.

National Organization on Male Survivor Victimization
5505 Connecticut Ave. NW
Washington, DC 20015-2601
1-800-738-4181
www.malesurvivor.org
A nonprofit organization dedicated to healing male survivors of sexual abuse.

VOICES in Action, Inc.
P.O. Box 148309
Chicago, IL 60614
773-327-1500
http://voices-action.org
Offers referrals to therapists, self-help groups, agencies, and legal resources.

Incest Resources, Inc. Cambridge Women's Center, 46 Pleasant St., Cambridge, MA 02139. Incest Resources publishes excellent low-cost literature on incest-related topics and offers a referral service.

Looking Up, P.O. Box K. Augusta, ME 04330. Looking Up provides referrals, low-cost conferences, workshops, and wilderness trips for non-offending survivors of child sexual abuse.

National Self-Help Clearinghouse, Graduate School, City University of New York, 35 West 42nd St., Rm. 1222, New York, NY 10036. Provides listing of self-help groups throughout the US.

PLEA (Prevention, Leadership, Education, and Assistance). P.O. Box 22, West Zia Road, Santa Fe, NM 87505. PLEA exclusively serves non-offending male survivors.

Keynotes, Seminars and Workshops

The goal of Cathy's distinctive presentations is to motivate individuals. Her intent is to encourage individuals to move beyond barriers, to move from low self-esteem to self-worth and to find purposeful fulfillment. Additionally, Cathy offers workshops and seminars for those in the human service, educational and law enforcement field.

Let us continue to work towards empowering individuals, families and communities with the hope that **WE** can pave the path to a healthier, happier future for the children and families of tomorrow.

For additional, specific information you can contact Cathy at:

Cathy Brochu
Espouse
P. O. Box 158
Jamesville, New York 13078-9536
E-mail: C.Brochu@juno.com

About The Author

Cathy Brochu no longer lives her life shamed, fearful, isolated or stripped of self-esteem. She speaks openly and honestly about her thirteen-year experience growing-up in an incestuous family. She has worked in the field of Child Welfare for more than thirty years. Working directly with victims, perpetrators and families. She has heard the endless stories and cries for help.

Cathy holds a Bachelor of Arts Degree and is trained in clinical hypnotherapy. In 1995, she was the recipient of the Women of Courage Award presented by the Syracuse Commission for Women for setting an example in over-coming the odds and speaking out about incest. She has been featured in newspapers throughout Central New York for her work in initiating and facilitating support groups for adult incest survivors. She also lectures to graduate students on the importance of knowing what to look for, what to ask, and what to do for a potential victim of child sexual abuse. She trains lay and professionals in the human service field in the area of child sexual abuse and has been the guest speaker for numerous nonprofit agencies. She has committed herself to empowering and strengthening individuals, families and communities to move beyond hopelessness to becoming leaders of their own lives.

Cathy is currently working on the third and final segment of her trilogy series, **Beyond Survival**.